Construction Law Reports
Volume 2

Construction Law Reports Volume 2

Edited by

Michael Furmston TD MA BCL LLM
Professor of Law, University of Bristol

and

Vincent Powell-Smith LLB (Hons) LLM DLitt
FCIArb
Sometime Lecturer in Law at the University of Aston Management Centre

The Architectural Press: London

First published in 1985 by the Architectural Press Ltd, 9 Queen Anne's Gate, London SW1H 9BY

British Library Cataloguing in Publication Data

Construction law reports.—Vol. 2–
    2. Building laws—England—Cases
    344.203'78624   KD1140.A7

ISBN 0–85139–781–6

Typeset by Phoenix Photosetting, Chatham in 11/13pt Baskerville
Printed in Great Britain by
Mackays of Chatham Ltd

Contents

Preface to the Series

It is one of the paradoxes of English law that although it develops through decided cases, it lacks any systematic programme for the reporting of cases. The construction industry has been particularly badly served in this respect, many important and interesting cases not being reported at all. The situation was greatly improved some years ago by the appearance of *Building Law Reports* but this excellent venture has not been able to close all the gaps in the system.

In particular we have been concerned that much more attention should be paid to the judgments of Official Referees. The Official Referees' court has now become in effect a specialist construction industry court, one of the few in the world. Most of the cases which come before Official Referees involve complex and technical issues of fact but many also involve difficult and important questions of law. It is important that the guidance which emerges from the court should be generally available in the industry and not confined to those who regularly practice before the court. The useful summaries which appear in the newly-launched *Construction Law Journal* bear witness to·this but we believe there will be an audience for a fuller report.

We plan to report all Official Referees' decisions containing points of construction law and appellate decisions therefrom. We hope to produce three volumes a year and as the series progresses to include earlier unreported decisions of general interest.

We are grateful to Maritz Vandenberg of Architectural Press Ltd for so readily taking our proposal on board, and we hope that this new series of law reports will be of interest not only to architects, quantity surveyors, engineers, contractors and sub-contractors, but also to members of the legal profession who are concerned with this vital area of the law.

Michael Furmston
Vincent Powell-Smith

The Official Referees and the Construction Industry

The post of Official Referee was created by the Judicature Act 1873. The first Official Referee was appointed in 1881. Under the Judicature Act 1884 actions could be referred to Official Referees for trial. Since 1st October 1982 actions may be commenced before Official Referees and cases compulsorily transferred to them.

The Official Referees have the status of Circuit Judges but are High Court Judges in function. There are at present six Official Referees, the senior of whom is usually styled "the Senior Official Referee" and they are based at the Law Courts in the Strand, although if the majority of witnesses live at a distance from London or in other special cases they will sit at a location which is convenient to the parties.

The Official Referees are not concerned exclusively with the construction industry, but form in effect a construction industry court because the industry is the major user of their services. The principal types of actions dealt with by the Official Referees are:

● Claims by and against architects, engineers, surveyors and other professionals in contract and in tort.

● Cases relating to building, civil engineering and construction generally, both in contract and in tort, including a great many cases involving the interpretation of the commonly used standard form construction contracts, such as those sponsored by the Joint Contracts Tribunal.

● Claims by and against local authorities relating to their statutory duties, especially those relating to the building regulations, public health legislation and building legislation generally.

● Claims relating to work done and materials supplied or services rendered.

Many of the cases are lengthy and complex and involve highly technical issues as well as difficult points of law, and lengthy cases are often divided into sub-trials. Under the Rules of the Supreme Court, Order 58, there is a limited right of appeal direct to the Court of Appeal from a decision of an Official Referee on a point of law and on a question of fact relevant to a charge of fraud or breach of professional duty, but not otherwise. In consequence, many cases of importance are finally disposed of by the Official Referees.

An important but little-known aspect of their functions is the duty imposed on them to sit as arbitrators to decide any matter referred to them by agreement between the parties: Arbitration Act 1950, s. 11. This service is little used in practice.

Architects – Delegation of duty – Duty of design a continuing obligation – Contractor's duty to warn of known defects in design – Implied
term – Liability for breach of building regulations – Joint and several
liability – Circuity of actions

EQUITABLE DEBENTURE ASSETS CORPORATION LTD

Plaintiffs

v

WILLIAM MOSS GROUP LTD AND OTHERS

Defendants

Queen's Bench Division
(Official Referee's Business)
27, 28, 29, 30 June 1983, 4, 5, 6, 7, 11, 12, 13,
14, 18, 19, 20, 21, 25, 26, 27, 28 July, 5, 6, 10,
11, 12, 13, 17, 18, 19, 20, 21, 24, 25, 27, 31
October, 1, 2, 7, 8, 9 November, 6 February 1984.

His Honour Judge John
Newey QC

An architect owes a duty to his client not only to design carefully but to keep the design
under review during erection.

The plaintiffs, developers, decided to build an office block in Ashford
on a site which was fully exposed to winds from the south. The defendants (Morgan) were the architects for the project; Moss were the main
contractors; Winmart were curtain walling consultants and Alpine
were nominated sub-contractors who designed, supplied and fixed curtain walls for the building. Alpine admitted liability to the plaintiffs
and went into liquidation.

Alpine's design of the curtain walling was defective and there were
defects in workmanship both by Alpine and by Moss. The building
leaked from an early stage. Alpine's attempts at remedial action were
unsuccessful.

HELD: (1) Morgan had a duty to design a watertight building and this
included a duty to redesign during construction as and when necessary.
They could not delegate this duty without the plaintiffs' consent. The

original decision to use curtain walling was not negligent but there had
been negligence in the selection of Alpine; in the acceptance of Alpine's
design; in the unsystematic use of the curtain walling consultant and in
supervision of the work.

(2) A term should be implied into the contract between Moss and the
plaintiffs that Moss would report design defects known to them. During
the course of the work it must have become apparent to Moss that the
design of the curtain walling was unbuildable and they should have
reported this.

(3) Alpine were nominated sub-contractors and not nominated
suppliers. Accordingly, Moss were also liable for Alpine's bad workmanship in carrying out works under the main contract (but *semble* not
for bad workmanship in remedial works since these works had not been
the subject of an architect's instruction).

(4) Moss were also liable for breach of the Building Regulations 1972.

(5) Winmart were not liable as they had done what they had been asked
to do carefully. They were not obliged officiously to advise or inspect
when not asked to do so.

HIS HONOUR JUDGE JOHN NEWEY QC: In this case by consolidated actions Equitable Debenture Assets Corporation Limited (whom I
will refer to as EDAC), owners of International House, Dover Place,
Ashford, Kent, claimed damages from John D. Morgan and David C.
Branch and from Morgan Branch Roberts (whom I will refer to col-
lectively as Morgan), architects of the building, William Moss Group Ltd
(Moss) contractors for the erection of the building, from Winmart Associates (Winmart), curtain walling consultants engaged by Morgan, from
Alpine Windows Ltd (Alpine), sub-contractors who designed, supplied
and fixed curtain walls for the building, and from M.J. Prater Asphalt
Company Ltd (Asphalt) who supplied and laid asphalt roof coverings.

EDAC alleged breaches of contract by each defendant except for
Winmart and negligence by each defendant. Morgan's, Moss's, Alpine's
and Winmart's breaches of duty are alleged to have resulted in curtain
walling which leaked and Morgan's, Moss's, and Asphalt's in roofs
which leaked.

Each defendant has filed a defence denying EDAC's allegations
and Morgan, Moss and Winmart also rely upon the Limitation Act
1939. Each defendant concerned with curtain walling and each concerned with roofs has served upon the others also concerned notices
claiming indemnity or contribution under the Law Reform (Married
Women and Tortfeasors) Act 1935, and each has denied the others'
allegations. Shortly before the actions were due to be tried Alpine
admitted liability to EDAC, but not the amount of damages recoverable
from them. Alpine also went into liquidation and have not taken any part

in the current proceedings. During the proceedings EDAC discontinued against Winmart and Moss withdrew its third party claim against Winmart.

Mr Stephen Desch for EDAC opened the case against all the defendants, but after his first two witnesses had given evidence, some of which related to roofs, Mr Brian Knight and Miss Jackson for Asphalt withdrew and the evidence and submissions were from then onwards confined to curtain walling. I am now giving judgment only in respect of liability in connection with curtain walling. I will (if necessary) deal with liability in relation to roofs after hearing further evidence and argument. Questions concerning damages will be the subject of later sub-trials.

Despite the limited scope of the present proceedings they have occupied 39 days, and involved consideration of plans, drawings, photographs, technical documents and about 2 500 pages of correspondence. Some documents included in the bundles were internal memoranda belonging to Alpine and as such were not evidence against other parties. I have visited on one occasion International House, accompanied by representatives of the parties.

The witnesses called on behalf of EDAC were: Mr A. L. Shane, a solicitor who qualified in 1933 and became personally involved in development in the mid-1950s, using a separate company for each project; Mr H. Barker, FRICS, who assisted Mr Shane full-time; Mr Roger Shane, a son of Mr Shane, born in about 1949, who helped him; and Dr W. A. Allan, CBE, FRIBA, and Mr B. Heath, MA, FRICE, who had prepared joint reports concerning the curtain walling and the responsibilities of those concerned and gave expert evidence. Proofs from nine witnesses dealing with the occurrence and location of leaks through the curtain walling were for present purposes accepted as being correct and the witnesses were not called.

Mr Igor Judge for Moss did not call Moss's site agent or agents or any witnesses of fact, but he called Mr Southgate, who had had many years experience of working for curtain walling suppliers and gave expert evidence as to curtain walling.

Mr Martin Collins called on behalf of Morgan: Mr D. A. Rae, ARIBA who was the project architect in charge of the building of International House; Mr D. Branch, a partner in Morgan, who was the partner responsible for the project; and Mr G. H. R. Hutton FRIBA, FRSA, who had prepared a report jointly with a Mr R. M. R. Rostron, MA, BArch, ARIBA, and who gave expert evidence with regard to curtain walling and the responsibilities of architects.

Mr Allan Moses called Mr N. B. Plough, the partner in Winmart most concerned with the project, who gave evidence both of fact and of an expert character; the latter based upon his long experience of curtain walling. The other partner in Winmart, Mr C. B. Sulston, has died.

Mr Shane impressed me as being competent and a person of integrity. He fully understood the financial and other hazards involved in carrying out development, he wanted value for money and was prepared to pay what was reasonable but not what he considered to be unreasonable.

Although naturally masterful, the captain of the team, Mr Shane was willing to repose trust in those who had worked for him in the past and would not readily withdraw such trust.

Mr Shane, like most of the other witnesses, was at times speaking of events which occurred 10 to 16 years ago and his health is not good. I think that there were occasions when his memory for dates went astray. Sometimes he telescoped two or more events together, but in the main I think that his evidence was reliable.

Mr Barker seemed to me to be careful and conscientious both in what he did and in the way in which he gave his evidence. I am sure that he did his best to tell me what happened. The same is I think true of young Mr Shane, who in the late 1960s found it embarrassing to raise points with those older and better qualified than himself, but who nonetheless was sufficiently determined to do so.

At times when Mr Rae was giving evidence I felt very sorry for him. I am sure that he is fundamentally honest and honourable, interested in the work of his profession, and probably good at much of it. On the other hand, I think that at material times he was a poor organiser and lacked the firmness of purpose and the assertiveness required for effective supervision of a large project. Probably he will have learned a great deal from the searing experience of this case. I found Mr Rae an unimpressive witness and particularly with regard to what he saw or did on site I fear that he must have suffered from what Mr Desch elegantly described as "merciful amnesia".

Mr Branch's evidence was relatively short and, so far as it went, impressively given. He is obviously a most experienced architect and I would think a much firmer character than Mr Rae. Unfortunately, he appeared not to have applied his mind to many problems which arose; he left matters to Mr Rae, even when it was clear that decisive action was required.

Mr Plough was clearly very knowledgeable about curtain walling and, therefore, well worth employing as a consultant. I have the impression, however, that he was somewhat of a muddler where business was concerned. He seems to have been taciturn at material times, but was voluble in the witness box. I have no doubt that Mr Plough endeavoured to tell me the truth, but his recollections are not always easy to reconcile with the contemporary letters written by Mr Sulston; in the event I do not think that the differences matter.

As to the experts, I found all their reports and evidence helpful.

They were generally agreed as to the direct causes of the leaks and their opinions as to responsibility tended to shade one into another. They disagreed as to whether at various stages parts of the curtain walling could have been retained or whether all had to be taken out and replaced.

I will state my main findings with regard to the facts as briefly as I can and usually without summarising rival evidence. I will then deal one by one with the issues which the parties have asked me to decide, but not always in the order in which they listed them.

In or about 1955 Mr Shane began to employ upon projects which he initiated Morgan as architects, Derek Lane & Associates (Lane) as quantity surveyors and Mr John Bunce as structural engineer. Mr Shane's policy was to build commercial properties, of a standard which the market required, with finance obtained on loan, and then to let them. He sought to keep maintenance costs to a minimum and to avoid disputes with tenants.

By the mid-1960s Mr Shane had undertaken about ten projects: curtain walling had been used on some of them, and on one at Harrow and one at Edgware had given rise to trouble on a fairly modest scale.

In about 1965 Lane brought to the attention of Mr Shane the site which became that of International House. The site was close to where it was expected that a new ring road for Ashford would connect with an approach road to the channel tunnel. The site was fully exposed to winds to the south as there were no hills between it and the sea and to the north the nearest hills were the North Downs.

Mr Shane was interested, Morgan prepared eighth-inch scale plans, which showed a 12-storey rectangular block and a 5-storey rect-angular block meeting at a right angle, made of reinforced concrete with curtain walls made of aluminium and glass on the longer eleva-tions. Those elevations were to the south and north of the larger block, called A, and the east and west of the smaller block B. Parapets would be provided around the tops of the blocks and also a caretaker's flat and boiler room on top of block A. Lane prepared estimates of construction costs and lettable areas. Applications for planning and office develop-ment permissions were sought and eventually obtained and the site was purchased by EDAC.

On 30 November 1967 there was a meeting between Mr Shane, Mr Barker, Mr Branch and Mr Lane. Mr Shane questioned the proposed use of curtain walling and mentioned his concern to avoid maintenance problems. Mr Shane referred to leaks at Harrow and Mr Barker to those at Edgware.

Mr Shane asked whether brick walling or concrete blocks could not be used. Mr Branch explained that bricks would be prohibitively expensive and that blocks would be unsightly when used externally. He explained that there would be blocks behind the glass cladding and gave an assurance that he would take special care with the design.

Mr Shane and Mr Barker were each expecting the new building to have a life of 70 or more years, but neither said so. Equally, Mr Branch did not state that the curtain walling would have to be renewed during the life of the building and Mr Barker believed that it would require cleaning only.

I do not think Mr Branch said at the meeting that he would employ a curtain walling consultant, but it was because of anxiety expressed at it that he soon afterwards contacted Winmart and sent to them copies of his drawings. In a letter of 1 December Mr Branch wrote to Mr Shane confirming that he would "be reconsidering the project in the light of the general uplift in office accommodation requirements and the prudent selection of planning materials, etc". In a letter to heating consultants of 5 January 1968 Mr Shane wrote "The site is in a cold corner of England and the building is tall and in an exposed position".

In 1968 Mr Plough prepared at Morgan's request a specification for the supply of curtain walling for Ashford. He also prepared a basic drawing of a part elevation for windows with structural elements. On 10 March 1969 Mr Plough revised the specification. Windows were to be supplied in mill finish aluminium alloy. It was stated that the site was "very exposed" and that winds equivalent to 80 mph were to be expected at first floor level and 100 miles per hour above that level. The supplier had to "guarantee that the installation offered was strong enough and will provide a completely watertight window wall".

On 8 March Mr Bunce wrote to Mr Barker drawing his attention to publications concerning wind loading and in somewhat convoluted language asking him to await Mr Branch's investigations before making progress with working drawings.

At a meeting in May Mr Shane finally appointed Morgan as architects for the project and stressed the need for careful supervision. On 8 May Mr Branch wrote to Mr Shane stating that he would be the partner in charge of the project, but the day-to-day running of it would be the responsibility of Mr Rae and that during the contract weekly visits would be made to the site.

Mr Shane said that during casual conversation Mr Branch had advised against the employment of a clerk of works. That may well have happened, but earlier in their relationship, as there had been no clerk of works on any of Mr Shane's projects. In a letter of 16 May Mr Shane agreed to a £100 per annum as travelling expenses "in view of (his) insistence that there be proper control of the contractor whilst he is on site".

Mr Branch took Mr Rae to Mr Shane's office to be introduced. Mr Roger Shane, speaking from personal experience, referred to trouble

2 ConLR   Equitable Debenture Assets Corporation Ltd v William Moss and Others   7

with tenants concerning leaks. Mr Branch told him that the matter could be safely left to Mr Rae.

Soon afterwards Mr R. Shane telephoned Mr Rae and sought indirectly to discover his experience of curtain walling. Mr Rae listened politely and said that he would provide particulars of a building with curtain walling which Mr R. Shane could view; Mr Rae provided particulars by letter of 25 June 1969.

On 4 July 1969 there was a meeting of all who were concerned with the development. The minutes prepared by Morgan record that "the architect informed the client that he had at his own expense obtained the services of a curtain walling consultant to ensure that the client obtained the best possible installation based on present codes of practice, regulations and sections." Both Mr Shane and Mr Barker found that reassuring. Mr Barker told me that he expected the consultant would provide a full service. Mr Roger Shane, who must have been looking at the Winmarts' drawing, asked that Morgan consider the proposed head detail from the point of view of water ingress.

On 23 July Mr Sulston wrote a somewhat confused letter to Lane apparently stating that the time had come when Winmart should have the opportunity of designing the whole window wall section. I do not know whether the letter was passed to Morgan.

On 10 September Mr Sulston in a letter for the attention of Mr Rae confirmed having handed to him full sized details of curtain walling and five copies of a specification and suggested four companies from whom tenders for the supply of curtain walling might be invited. The copy of the specification contained the same warning as to exposure and wind speeds as before and details of requirements. Morgan invited tenders from three of the companies, namely, Aygee (Metal Windows) Ltd, Gardner Aluminium Windows and Crittall-Hope Ltd. Each submitted a detailed tender, but Gardner's in particular gave design wind speeds and calculations based upon them. Later Gardner's invited attendance at a water and air infiltration test of a proposed double-hung window.

On 30 September Winmart presented a bill for "design and development time . . . including working drawings and specification", which, characteristically I fear, Morgan overlooked.

After correspondence and discussion between EDAC and Morgan during the autumn of 1969 Mr Shane decided that the companies nominated as sub-contractors to be employed by the head contractor upon the project should be required to enter into collateral agreements with EDAC in a form newly introduced by the RIBA (what I will call a direct warranty). Mr Shane left to Morgan the selection of sub-contractors. After discussion EDAC decided that sub-contractors should not be asked to provide performance bonds.

Morgan submitted the tenders to Winmart, who after due consideration of them on 25 February 1970 advised that the lowest might be accepted. Before, however, Morgan could act on that advice and could also, as they intended, obtain a tender for the main contract from Moss, Mr Shane decided to bring matters to a stop. The plan for a channel tunnel had been cancelled and the demand for offices seemed uncertain.

In May 1971 when the project was still in abeyance, Alpine wrote to Lane requesting that they be included among the tenderers for curtain walling. Alpine had been incorporated in 1968 and had as its sales manager Mr Trotman, who had previously been with Aygee.

Towards the end of 1971 Mr Shane revived the project and wanted it to proceed with speed. Moss were approached and on 7 January 1972 Lane invited the original tenderers for sub-contract work to submit fresh tenders. Unfortunately, in the meanwhile Aygee had gone into liquidation and Gardner's did not in the event submit a tender. Mr Rae approached Alpine's and E. D. Hinchcliffe & Sons Ltd and, as he told me, in order to save time asked them to collect from Morgan's office copies of the drawings and specification prepared by Winmart.

During the period between September 1969 and January 1972 there was a major development with regard to curtain walling, namely the issue in March 1971 of the British Standards Institution's *Draft for Development 4*(DD4). The draft set standards to be achieved on testing for windows exposed to different grades of exposure, which were recognised in terms of three-second gust speeds. There were three main grades: sheltered up to 40 metres per second; moderate up to 45 m/s; and severe up to 50 m/s and above. A map of the United Kingdom showed basic wind speeds, with Ashford in a 38 to 40 m/s band. For windows more than 10 m high, basic speeds had to be multiplied by corrective factors, depending on height and category, "open country with no obstacles" being the worst, to arrive at appropriate values. Critical values were given as 45 m/s for moderate and 50 m/s for severe. Where windows were to be within 3 m of an exposed corner it was recommended that a grade of exposure one higher than would normally be assumed should be taken. The draft made recommendations with regard to testing, but of a somewhat tentative character.

No doubt Alpine had Morgan's drawings of 1969, but I am uncertain whether they collected Winmart's drawing and specification. They made calculations which were disclosed on discovery and which, as is clear from Dr Allan's and Mr Heath's report, were wrong as to wind loading. On 3 March they submitted tenders for two different designs accompanied by schematic drawings, which showed double hung sash vision windows above opaque coloured spandrel panels, all set in aluminium ladder-like frames.

In Alpine's quotation they stated that the scheme which they proposed was one of which they had had experience on an exposed site in the Southampton Dock area, being an office block 6 and 11 storeys high. They offered to provide the name of the architect concerned. Mr Rae obtained the name of architect who said that no problems had arisen. Unfortunately, Mr Rae did not ask the extent to which curtain walling had been used nor go to see the building; if he had done so, he would have discovered that curtain walling was used only to a limited extent and on lower floors only. Alpine's tender was obviously much less detailed than say Gardner's earlier one.

Mr Rae contacted Winmart, who had not been consulted about the project since 1969. He did not ask them for their confidential opinion of Alpine, but convened a meeting attended by Mr Trotman as well as by Mr Plough on 13 March. At that meeting Mr Plough was given a brief opportunity to examine Alpine's tenders without drawings and he did not make any positive comments with regard to them.

On 6 April Mr Rae asked Alpine to confirm that their window wall installation conformed with Winmart's specification, which he enclosed. Alpine did not reply and Mr Rae did not send them a reminder.

On 7 April there was another meeting attended by Mr Rae, Mr Plough and Mr Trotman. At it Mr Plough mentioned the desirability of fire breaks in the curtain walling, but very little else seems to have been said. On 26 April there occurred yet another meeting, attended by the same persons. Mr Plough said that drawings were produced, but that they related only to part of the installation. By that time Mr Rae had received rival tenders to Alpine's from Crittall-Hope and Hinchcliffe, but Mr Plough was not consulted about them.

On 1 May Mr Sulston wrote to Morgan protesting that Winmart had not been given an opportunity to update their specification and stating that they did not know what documents Morgan had issued and that they felt that their services at that stage would be of little value. It is surprising that Mr Plough had not said as much at any of the meetings.

On 2 May Mr Branch replied to Mr Sulston saying that Mr Plough had been invited to Morgan's office to review their specification and to give his comments concerning Alpine whom Mr Branch described as having "put in a good tender on the basis of [Mr Plough's specification]". Mr Branch plainly believed that Alpine had had a copy of the specification and did not know that they had not replied to Mr Rae's letter of 6 April.

Mr Sulston responded on the 3 May saying that Winmart would be pleased to service the job, but would like to call a meeting as soon as possible with the successful tenderer to go through their scheme drawings. Mr Branch did not write back saying "please hold the meeting".

On 1 May a contract had been made between EDAC and Moss for erecting the office development at Ashford. The contract was in the JCT Standard Form of Building Contract, private edition with quantities 1963 edition (July 1971 revisions), subject to certain amendments. I will refer to it as the head contract. Morgan were named as the architects.

On 16 May Morgan instructed Moss to accept Alpine's revised tender; in substance Morgan nominated Alpine as sub-contractors. It was the first time that Moss had known of Alpine in this context. Moss had a right if the nomination was under clause 27(a) to make "reasonable objection" to the nomination, but would obviously have been beset by practical difficulties in doing so at short notice. Moss gave notice to Alpine of their intention to place the sub-contract with them.

On or about 16 May Moss sent to EDAC for signature a Direct Warranty Contract between themselves and Alpine in the Standard Employer/Sub-contractor (1971) Form. Under it Alpine warranted, *inter alia*, that they had exercised or would exercise all reasonable care and skill in:

(a) The design of the sub-contract works insofar as the sub-contract works have been or will be designed by the sub-contractor; and

(b) The selection of materials and goods for the sub-contract works insofar as such materials and goods have been or will be selected by the sub-contractor.

Neither Mr Shane nor Mr Barker had heard of Alpine, but Morgan had been authorised to select sub-contractors and Mr Shane signed the direct warranty.

On 30 May there was a long meeting between Mr Rae, Mr Powell and Mr Trotman. Alpine's drawings of 21 April 1972 were produced and contained some information as to the details of Alpine's design. Mr Plough pointed out that there were no expansion joints in the mullions shown and that the type of spigot to be used to splice together mullions made in sections was not stated. He suggested various changes.

Mr Plough expected that there would be further design meetings and that he would be able to participate in the preparation of working drawings.

On 7 July there was a sub-contractors' meeting attended by Mr Branch and Mr Rae, by representatives of Moss, by Alpine's designer Mr Theobald, and others.

According to the minutes Mr Theobald mentioned that he was experiencing difficulty in producing a satisfactory detail in both the sill and head of the curtain walling, the architect (meaning in fact Mr Rae) made suggestions, and Mr Theobald was instructed to ensure "his revised details and, indeed, all details" were checked and approved by

Mr Plough. Mr Theobald was also to furnish Mr Plough with "the Test Report on the curtain walling and to ensure that Mr Plough (was) satisfied with the performance figures". Mr Plough, who had not been invited to the meeting, was not sent a copy of the Minutes and did not know that Alpine was expected to contact him.

On 17 August Mr Rae received further details of Alpine's installations. The details were not sent to Mr Plough, but Mr Rae whose formal training as an architect included some study of curtain walling and who had had experience of it on other buildings, checked them himself, taking about 1½ days to do so.

About the middle of September Alpine telephoned Mr Plough and asked him to visit their works in order to check their working drawings and to agree dimensions. On 20 September Mr Plough visited the works, was shown drawings by Mr Trotman and was asked to approve them. Mr Plough considered that he had been excluded from any part in working out the drawings, became angry, refused to look at the drawings and after speaking to Mr Trotman, left. Mr Plough wrote a letter to Mr Rae dated 22 September; beginning at the second paragraph the letter read:

"In view of the very loose and to us unsatisfactory arrangement under which you would seem to wish to use our consultancy service we cannot accept this responsibility or continue on this basis. To explain our position more clearly: for our services to be of technical value to you and in our mutual best interests it is vital that a close liaison be maintained during the development of the details and the period of the contract. For over three months we have had no requests from you to attend any discussions regarding the windows. We have not been provided with any of your working drawings or information relating to them. We do not know if approval has been received from the District Surveyor regarding the method proposed for fixing the curtain walling to the structure of the building. In conclusion we would respectfully point out, when you give your general approval to window drawings it should be subject to agreement of dimensions between the main contractor and with their manufacturer. You should also request confirmation with the window manufacturer that the window installation will be completely watertight."

Mr Rae thought Mr Plough's letter strange, since Mr Plough had seen Alpine's tenders and had not objected to them. He passed the letter to Mr Branch who arranged a meeting for 26 September. What was agreed at the meeting was set out in a letter by Mr Branch written on the following day, although dated the 26th, which read:

"Thank you for your letter of the 22nd September addressed to Mr Brian Rae in connection with the above Contract, and for attending a meeting at this Office this afternoon to discuss the present situation. I would confirm that it was agreed that you would provide a watching brief on the curtain wall contract, attending meetings when requested and commenting upon details when requested, and you will attend with us a simulated water test with the sub-Contractor's Works when ready and inspect work on site during progress of the sub-Contract, when requested. For this service we will pay your fees on a day or part-time basis.''

The fact that Mr Plough had not checked Alpine's drawings does not seem to have concerned either Mr Rae or Mr Branch. He was not asked to carry out a check. On 26 September a sub-contract was made between Moss and Alpine.

On 2 October 1972 Mr Rae wrote to Alpine asking for an early window and spandrel panel water test, so that any variations necessitated by it could be incorporated without affecting the programme of work. Mr Rae raised 14 other points, all of which, according to Mr Plough had been discussed at the meetings attended by him. Rather oddly, in view of Winmart's limited future role, the letter stated that Mr Plough would like to know the pointing mastic which Alpine proposed to use. No copy of the letter was sent to Mr Plough.

At a sub-contractors' meeting on 13 October, Alpine was asked to supply finalised drawings immediately. On 17 October Mr Trotman replied to Mr Rae's letter of 2 October; passages in Mr Trotman's letter could be read as meaning that Alpine had been in recent contact with Mr Plough but in fact, they had not.

On 19 October Mr Theobald called on Mr Rae and handed to him copies of Alpine's final installation drawings 798/1–7. Mr Rae, as he reported at the site meeting next day, checked the drawings and made various amendments. On 23 October Mr Theobald sent to Mr Rae drawings 798/8 and 9 with a request that he check details and dimensions shown. On 25 October Mr Rae approved the drawings 798/1–7, upon which certain revisions had been noted. He must have subsequently approved the two later drawings, for on 3 November Mr Rae informed a site meeting that he had instructed Alpine to make a general issue of their drawings.

Alpine sent copies to Morgan who themselves made a general issue of them prior to a site meeting on 17 November. A formal issue of Alpine's drawings to Moss provided Moss with their first opportunity of seeing them. Winmart were not included among those to whom Alpine's drawings were sent. They were sent copies of minutes to site meetings, but not asked to do anything as the result.

On 14 December Mr Rae agreed to a request from Alpine that they be allowed to use sub-contract labour, namely, Lux-Fix Installations

Ltd, to carry out work on site necessary in order to attach Alpine's pre-fabricated units to the building. Mr Rae had not made any enquiries about Lux-Fix and Moss's consent was not sought nor were they consulted.

On or about 1 January 1973 Alpine's units began to arrive on site and Lux-Fix commenced installation. About a week later a test of a sash unit was carried out by Mr Theobald at Alpine's premises and using their rig in the presence of Mr Rae and of Mr Perry, an employee of Winmart, who was substituting for Mr Plough. Mr Rae gave evidence that Mr Perry had no criticisms of the rig or of the tests and that the test went off satisfactorily. Mr Rae did not request a written report from Mr Perry, but Mr Perry made one to Mr Plough in, which in substance he reported that Mr Theobald had taken as standard what would in DD4 terms have been "moderate" grade and that the unit had met that standard. Alpine could not at their premises have tested two or more units and the fittings between them at the same time and, although such a test could have been carried out by the construction of a special rig, that would have been very expensive and was not suggested by anyone.

The Alpine curtain walling units which Lux-Fix had begun to instal each consisted of double-hung sash, sliding windows on framed 4 mm visioned glass and permanently fixed framed grey toughened 6 mm glass spandrel panels, together set in storey-height mullions formed in pairs but spliced together by spigots. There were transoms at the heads of the window and of the spandrel attached to the mullions by self-tapping screws and a snap-in bead at the bottom of the spandrel. There were quarter-inch movement joints between mullions. The glazing was by preformed gaskets and sub-frames were provided with brush seals to the mullions. Apart from mild steel spigots and stainless steel screws, the only metal used was aluminium.

On site Lux-Fix had to apply sealing compound (a sealant) to the internal bases of butt joints between mullions and transoms, and to bed the snap-in bead, the spandrel frame and all edge sections up to movement levels on the mullions in the sealant.

Units were attached to the structure of the building by mild steel cleats and unistruts, gaps being filled with shims. At corners half mullions were secured to timber attached to brick walls facing the concrete structure, with vertical damp proof courses in between bricks and structure.

The arrangement for protecting the heads of the curtain walling involved linking them with the parapets by means of a continuous aluminium fascia around slabs protruding from the tops of the blocks on which the parapets rested. Each parapet consisted of a concrete skin and a flint lime brick external skin with a 1½ in cavity between, with a coping on top. In the cavities there was to be a dpc leading water past the top of the fascia into weep holes in the outer skins. Sealant was to be applied at the junctions of the double-hung sash frames and the fascia and where the fascia met the outer skin, but not so as to block weep holes.

Figures 3, 4, 5, 6 and 7 of Dr Allan's and Mr Heath's report and illustrative drawings produced by Mr Desch during his opening and referred to frequently throughout the trial show clearly and more fully than I have been able to describe in words Alpine's design.

In the weeks and months which followed Moss proceeded with the erection of the main structure of the building and provided scaffolding around it. Lux-Fix worked from both inside the building and from scaffolding. When roof levels were reached Moss's own workforce constructed the parapets and dealt with the flanks.

As promised to Mr Shane, Mr Rae paid weekly visits to the site and walked about it, sometimes accompanied by Moss's site agent, a representative of Lane or Mr Bunce and sometimes alone. He went on to the scaffolding. He told me that on the lower block B he remembered seeing fixers working sealants into the mullions and also applying them elsewhere. He saw sealants on site ready for use. He noticed holes in sashes and spoke to Mr Legett, Alpine's foreman who made periodic visits to the site, about them. Mr Rae did not specifically remember seeing sealants being used on the taller block A. On Mr Rae's visits he usually spent most of the day on the site, but part of the time was devoted to a site meeting. Mr Rae did not make surprise inspections, but Mr Branch did from time to time, but often, however, on Sundays, when work was not in progress.

Plainly, both Mr Rae and Mr Branch thought the installation of the curtain walls was being performed correctly. Neither a representative of Moss or anyone else said anything to make them believe the contrary. No one said that the fixers were having difficulty in fulfilling the requirements of Alpine's drawings. There were problems about waxing, taping and stacking of components, which are no longer, I think, material. At a site meeting on 7 April 1973 Mr Rae instructed Moss to ensure that anti-condensation channels were free of mortar droppings and builder's rubbish prior to the fixing of infill panels. At a meeting on 28 September Mr Rae complained of the manner of fixing the damp proof course in one section of the parapet and required that section of the wall to be taken down and the dpc renewed. Other matters concerning curtain walling arose from time to time, but by October Morgan was principally concerned with matters unconnected with both curtain walling and the parapets and made a complaint about them to Moss's Head Office. On 2 November Morgan complained specifically with regard to site supervision.

It would seem that it was early in October that water penetration in the curtain walling first occurred. Moss complained to Alpine on 9 October. At the end of the month Alpine obtained an estimate from Douglas & Gavin, sealant applicators, for applying a small triangular section fillet each side of the mullions for the full length of the double hung sliding sashes. This marked the beginning of Alpine's efforts to make the curtain walling already installed watertight by the external application of sealants, which had never been envisaged as part of the design.

By February 1974 installation was almost complete but leaks kept occurring and Moss began to make frequent complaints to Alpine of badly fitting windows. Mr Rae did not notice the leaks at first, but at a site meeting 16 August, when Moss reported various defects in the curtain walling without mentioning leaks, he gave instructions that Moss should take them up with Alpine and obtain Alpine's assurance that the curtain walling was in no way faulty.

On 21 August Alpine and Lux-Fix carried out by themselves a water test on part of the curtain walling and decided that weather bars were required to prevent water penetration of the heads of the double hung sashes and that polysulphuric bandage type joints should be used to prevent penetration through the expansion joints.

In late August Mr Barker, who had noted references to curtain walling in the site minutes, reminded Mr Branch that EDAC had drawn Morgan's attention particularly to the necessity for extreme care and close supervision in connection with curtain walling. Mr Branch assured him that the consultant employed to advise on the detailing of the curtain walling would be making a careful inspection. In a letter of 29 August Mr Barker asked that he might be present at the inspection.

Except for sending copies of site minutes and possibly a letter of 21 May, enclosing copies of other letters, Morgan had not been in touch with Winmart since January 1973. At no time had Mr Plough been asked to attend meetings or to comment upon details as contemplated when the watching brief was agreed. On 11 September, however, Mr Rae wrote to Mr Plough requesting him to carry out an investigation of the curtain walling and give his comments, so that Morgan could take action.

Mr Plough replied to Mr Rae on 16 September and, after complaining about the manner in which Winmart had been used, said that he would inspect the curtain walling at 10.30 on 19 September, but asked that Alpine's working drawings and tender documents be available for him.

Mr Rae wrote to Mr Barker on 18 September informing him of the inspection next morning. Mr Barker said that that was the only notice which he received and that on receiving it on the morning of the 19th he set out for Ashford but could not arrive until midday.

In the meanwhile, Mr Rae, Mr Plough and Alpine's represenative met on site. Despite his request Mr Plough was not provided with Alpine's drawings and since the scaffolding had been removed and there was no safety cradle available he was obliged to inspect the curtain walling from inside the building only.

Alpine offered to carry out remedial works, which they had thought necessary after their water test. They also offered to apply a sealant round the spandrels and to fit sash stop and joint plates where missing. Their offers were accepted. Mr Plough recommended that tolerances should be checked on mullions.

When Mr Plough was leaving the building, he met Mr Barker. They introduced themselves to each other and Mr Plough made some non-committal comments.

At a site meeting on the following day Moss stated that they had been informed by Alpine that the rectification work "necessitated due to a design error" would be completed in four weeks. By letter of 23 September Mr Plough recorded what had happened at the meeting on the 19th and ended with the words:

"For any further comments on the curtain walling construction you may require it will be necessary to provide me with the window manufacturer's working drawings".

Morgan did not reply.

Although Alpine's remedial measures plainly constituted changes in design, Morgan did not issue any instructions under the head contract authorising them.

Alpine by sub-contractors carried out remedial measures which they had promised between 1 November 1974 and 18 August 1975, which was, of course, considerably longer than four weeks. Unfortunately, they failed to prevent leaks, and Alpine therefore tried again using mastic sealants only between 7 October and 7 November 1975. On their second attempt failing, they made a third attempt to use mastic between 21 November and 22 December 1975.

Morgan took no initiative of their own, while these attempts were being made. This was, they say, because they believed that for them to issue instructions might prejudice EDAC's rights under the direct warranty.

Towards the end of November 1975 Mr Branch telephoned Mr Plough and asked him to attend a meeting at Ashford on 4 December. Mr Plough replied on 27 November, asking that Mr Branch should brief him before the meeting as to what he required him to report on. Mr Branch replied on 1 December saying that he would like a report regarding Alpine's remedial proposals. Mr Plough attended the meeting which was with Alpine and on 4 December submitted a report recording what had been said, but not containing any opinions of his own.

In early January 1976 Moss had pressed Morgan to issue a certificate of practical completion in respect of the contract. Mr Rae was inclined to do so, although the curtain walling had not been tested and there were other matters outstanding, but he was persuaded to issue what purported to be one only in a qualified form drafted by Mr Shane, excluding curtain walling and asphalt roofs.

On 20 January, the day before the issue of the certificate, Alpine wrote to Morgan claiming that the last remedials had been successful, but, alas, the weather soon proved them wrong; the curtain walling leaked once more. Alpine made a fourth attempt at stopping leaks between 5 March and 21 June 1976; without, as usual, any instructions from Morgan.

On 19 October Mr Barker wrote to Mr Rae complaining of what he described as his "very hit and miss method of dealing with a serious basic defect". The use of the words "basic defect" show, I think, that EDAC realised that what was wrong with curtain walling could not be attributed exclusively to workmanship. Mr Barker went on to write that "at best there is no certainty as to how long this makeshift remedy will last" and that EDAC were strongly concerned that "an independent survey should be made of the whole of the curtain walling with a view to establishing what caused the trouble and the best long term remedy". Morgan were asked to recommend a competent firm of consultants.

Mr Rae wrote separate letters to Mr Barker and Mr Shane both on 28 October 1976. In the first of them Mr Rae wrote "We must allow Messrs Alpine to proceed with their proposed rectification work as to delay acceptance could be construed as preventing them from executing their contractual commitment", and then recommended Mr Plough as a suitable consultant. In the second letter Mr Rae wrote "it would be imprudent of us to suggest to the main contractor that he should advise his sub-contractors to adopt a particular course of remedial work. The reason being that this could absolve the main contractor from any further responsibility should the work fail".

Mr Shane and Mr Barker did not make any comment upon Mr Rae's views of the law. They believed that Mr Plough had been actively concerned throughout the works and did not, therefore, regard him as being sufficiently independent to instruct. Such was their faith in Morgan and Mr Shane's feeling of friendship with Mr Branch that no new initiative was taken.

Between 29 November and 9 May 1977 Alpine made yet another attempt to stop the leaks by the application of sealant. On the latter date Mr Rae made an inspection and on or about 9 June he issued a certificate of practical completion in respect of curtain walling and roofing. Leaks soon resumed and have continued ever since.

Early in December 1978 Mr Shane met Mr Woods of Moss who

told him that the defects in the curtain walling were of design. Mr Shane put the suggestion to Mr Branch in a letter of 4 December, who replied on 19 December that "workmanship played a part".

On 22 December Mr Barker had a conversation with Mr Rae, of which Mr Barker made a contemporaneous note. Mr Barker confirmed the accuracy of his note, part of which read "Mr Rae informed me that he had also complained on a number of occasions . . . of the skimped and unsatisfactory workmanship of the operatives employed by Alpine Windows Ltd who had only been concerned at getting through the job as quickly as possible". In evidence Mr Rae agreed that he had spoken of workmanship with Mr Barker, but denied that he had said all that Mr Barker attributed to him. I think that Mr Barker's account of what Mr Rae said is substantially correct.

Mr Shane asked Morgan to let him see Mr Plough's reports; obviously expecting more substantial documents than those written by Mr Plough to which I have referred. None was disclosed at that time.

The first independent inspection aimed at discovering the causes of the leaks was carried out by Dr Allan in company with Mr Pennington in March 1980. There was a further inspection by Dr Allan and Mr Heath in November 1981. Since then each of the experts has carried out at least one further inspection, apart from their visit with me. Parts of the curtain wall were for the first time opened up and from what was then discovered about the presence or absence of sealants, the presence or absence of spigots and screws, the condition of the dpc and the parapet cavities, the presence of water in the fascia and other places, the number of shims and other matters, individual experts drew inferences, now set out in their reports, which are overwhelming to the effect that similar conditions exist everywhere else. I think that the places opened up were representative and I draw the same inferences as do the experts.

After considering the experts' reports and their evidence I find that:
1. Alpine's design of the curtain walling for International House was based on what is known as the front sealed principle, that is to say total exclusion of water, and not of the rain screen principle, which allows water pass through an outer skin and then drains it away. There was, therefore, no second line of defence, which would have provided satisfactorily for collecting water in condensation gutters and draining it out of the building.
2. Because of the location of International House and the openness of the surrounding country, the curtain walling was certain to be subject to high wind loading. In terms of DD4 very many of the units should because of their height and/or closeness to corners have met or nearly met the requirements for severe grade.
3. The framework of the curtain walling units was flimsy and not sufficiently robust for International House. It vibrated readily in strong

winds. The sash windows within it deflect easily on light manual pressures. In terms of DD4, as was in fact shown by a test conducted by the British Standards Institution after installation of the curtain walling had been commenced, the Alpine unit was only up to sheltered grade.

4. The system did not provide satisfactorily for thermal movement in the framework; the manner of fixing mullion halves to spigots and cleats was certain to result in and did result in stresses causing slack joints and distortion of members.

5. Initially the movement joints were not shielded, so that water entered the mullions. Mastic bandages added as part of remedial works proved inadequate.

6. Some movement joints were omitted.

7. The brush seals to the mullions were unable adequately to exclude water; some were omitted altogether.

8. The applications of sealants to the mullions, transoms, snap-in beads and spandrel frames was certain to be difficult; checking that the work had been done properly was also certain to be difficult; in many places sealants were not applied at all and in many others they were not applied properly.

9. Numerous screw and bolt holes in the aluminium were left unplugged and able to admit water.

10. In many places because of inaccuracies in the concrete structure of the building large numbers of shims had to be used when securing the curtain walling to it.

11. The damp proof courses in the parapets were not carried over the tops of the fascia so that water was able to enter the fascia. Vertical damp proof courses were sometimes omitted at corners.

12. Mastic applied as a dam against water ingress blocked the weep holes at the bottom of the walls.

13. Introduction of angles and repeated application of mastic externally in attempts to stop leaks were only partially successful. The appearance of the mastic is unsightly and since it is fully exposed to sunlight and to rain and wind, even if it had been wholly effective, it would not have continued to have been for long.

The various ways in which water enters International House are shown in detail on figures 8–16 to Dr Allan's and Mr Heath's report and in the EDAC illustrative drawings.

To see clear evidence of leaks it is not necessary to visit International House when it is raining; numerous stains caused by damp can be seen on the walls at any time.

On 9 January 1980 EDAC issued a writ against Alpine and Moss and on 12 May 1980 issued a writ against Morgan. The claim against Morgan was amended on 25 February 1983 and again on 22 April 1983;

leave for each amendment was given on terms that time be deemed to run from the date of it, as was possible under the Limitation Act 1939: *Lipton's Cash Registers* v *Hugin* [1982] 1 All ER 395, Judge Hawser, QC.

The statement of claim as originally delivered alleged, *inter alia*, that Morgan was retained to "design and supervise" the works and that their manner of doing so was in breach of contract and/or negligent. By the first amendment failure to redesign was alleged.

The first of the agreed issues is:

What degree of rain penetration prevention should have been achieved by:
(a) *The curtain walling?*
(b) *The vertical abutment to the curtain walling?*
(c) *The parapet?*
(d) *The fascia?*

International House was designed and built for use as offices. Everyone concerned with it must inevitably have foreseen that within it executive and clerical work would be carried out, meetings held, visitors received, books, records and documents kept and electrical and other office equipment used. Everyone must have foreseen that occupants of the offices would wish to use all of them, including parts immediately adjacent to the outer walls. Everyone would have known that the offices were intended for sale or for letting to tenants, whose standard of requirements would be those appropriate for large, new offices on the outskirts of a country town, but not those appropriate for a prestige headquarters in central London.

In my opinion the curtain walling had ordinarily to prevent leaks from occurring even after prolonged wind and rain, but that a very occasional minor leak would have had to be tolerated.

Since penetration by water of the parapet, fascia and vertical abutments to the curtain walling could each cause or contribute to water entering the interior of the building from the curtain walling, I think that each should have excluded rain to the same degree as the curtain walling.

These conclusions accord with those which I reached in relation to water penetration of aluminium framed windows in a hospital in *Holland Hannen & Cubitts (Northern) Ltd* v *WHTSO* (1981) 18 BLR 80 at p 115, to which references were made in argument.

The second issue is:

What degree of rain penetration (if any) has each of the foregoing allowed during what period or periods?

I think that the curtain walling, vertical abutments, parapet and fascia have each contributed to water entering the building to an unacceptable degree. The first leaks were in October 1983 and since the summer of 1984 they have been almost continual, except during dry weather. On every occasion there have been leaks through the curtain walling and from the dates when the parapets were completed there must also have been leaks through them and through the fascia above them. Leaks through the vertical abutments occurred, but when I do not know.

The third issue is:

Has such penetration been due to any and, if so, what defects of:
(a) *Design, and*
(b) *Workmanship*
at what material time or times and in particular since 9 May 1977?

I will deal first with design, then workmanship, then causation and finally dates of occurrence.

As to design, in my opinion much the serious defect in design was that the curtain walling was not sufficiently robust for International House because of its height and its very exposed location. Adoption of the front sealed principle was not in itself wrong, provided that the outer face of the curtain walling would be able to prevent all except very occasional minor leaks. Unfortunately, because of the lightness of and lack of strength in the aluminium framework, it was certain that vibration due to wind and rain and the results of ordinary opening and closing of windows would cause it to become misshapen to such an extent as to admit rain. Once water had passed the outer face, there was no provision for draining it away again.

Lack of proper provision for thermal movement and the methods of fixing prescribed were certain to result in strains upon the framework, which again would cause it to become misshapen and to admit water. Selection of brush seals which were inadequate to exclude water was a further design mistake.

I think that if implementation of part of a design requires work to be carried out on site, the designer should ensure that the work can be performed by those likely to be employed to do it, in the conditions which can be foreseen, by the exercise of the care and skill ordinarily to be expected of them. If the work would demand exceptional skill, and particuarly if it would have to be performed partly from scaffolding and often in windy conditions, then the design will lack what the experts in evidence described as "buildability".

Similarly, I think that if a design requires work to be carried out on site in such a way that those whose duty it is to supervise it and/or check that it has been done will encounter great difficulty in doing so, then the design will again be defective. It may perhaps be described as lacking "supervisability".

In my view, applications of sealant in accordance with the design were possible in this case. A person with Mr Plough's experience, acting carefully and with determination, could no doubt have carried them out correctly. However, I think that ordinary fitters, even if they were not, as described by Mr Rae on 22 December 1979, "getting through the job as quickly as possible", could not have been expected, or relied upon, especially in view of working conditions, to do the job properly. It follows that in my opinion the design did not meet the requirements of buildability.

On the other hand, I think that the application of sealants was supervisable. I think that a competent supervisor, whether a foreman, site agent, or an architect, could with determination and persistence have discovered whether the sealants were being applied adequately or not.

The design of the vertical abutments and of the fascia could certainly have been improved, or an alternative for them provided, but on balance I do not hold that it was defective. I think that the design of the parapet and its connection with the fascia should be regarded as satisfactory.

The five times attempted remedial works were based almost entirely on the external application of sealants and as such were never likely to succeed, at any rate permanently. I think therefore that they must all be regarded as defective in design. A policy of patching was not good enough; a completely new solution to the curtain walling problem was required, necessitating a new design.

As to workmanship, I think that omission of movement joints, failure to ensure the presence of brush seals and leaving screw holes unplugged were all defects of workmanship. I think that if the fitters had reported that they found themselves unable to apply sealants in accordance with Alpine's drawings they could not have been criticised on that account, but, since they made no such report, but instead simply did not apply them properly, they were in that respect also guilty of bad workmanship.

The excessive use of shims was, I think, primarily the result of inaccuracies in the reinforced concrete structure of the building, for which the fitters cannot be blamed.

The incorrect fixing of damp proof courses in the parapet walls and the blocking of weep holes at their base was caused by Moss's employees' bad workmanship.

Much of the application of sealants during the remedial works was so poorly done that I think it has to be characterised as bad workmanship, although I feel some sympathy for the workmen, who must have experienced an ever increasing feeling of hopelessness!

Next *causation*. In my opinion even had there been perfect workmanship, the design of the curtain walling would have resulted in it leaking. Bad workmanship caused the curtain walling to leak more than it would otherwise have done, but, even with good workmanship, the curtain walling would have leaked to a wholly unacceptable degree.

Bad workmanship could have been made good to a large extent: I think that the bad design could never have been remedied except by taking out most of the existing curtain walling and replacing it by something better.

Unless the curtain walling had been designed on the rain screen principle, leaks from the parapet into the heads of the curtain walling were certain to enter the building. Since, as I have said, adoption of the front seal principle cannot by itself be faulted, it follows that these particular leaks must be attributed exclusively to defective workmanship.

External application of sealants could not have stopped leaks completely, but better workmanship would have reduced them temporarily.

With regard to *dates of occurrence*. The first leak of October 1973 may have been due either to the defective design or to bad workmanship, or to a combination of both; it is impossible for me to be certain. Since about February 1974 leaks have in my view been due both to design and workmanship.

The fourth issue is prefaced with the general questions:

Which defendants were responsible for such defects and in what respects were they so responsible?

and then goes on to pose groups of questions in relation to each defendant. I will take all questions relating to a defendant at the same time.

Questions concerning Morgan read:

(a) (i) *What design duty did Morgan owe to EDAC?*

(ii) *Was it increased or decreased by any (and if so what) factors?*

(iii) *Were Morgan in breach of such duty and in what respect?*

(c) (i) *During and after the installation of the curtain walling what duties of inspection and/or supervision and/or investigation (by themselves and/or others and which) did Morgan owe to EDAC?*

(ii) *Were such duties increased or decreased by any (and if so, what) factors?*

(iii) *Were Morgan in breach of any (and which) such duties and, if so, in what respects?*

(h) (i) *Did Morgan owe EDAC a duty of care to make use of Winmart's services in respect of:*

(1) *Design?*

(2) *Inspection and/or supervision and/or investigation during and after the installation of curtain walling?*

(ii) *If so were Morgan in breach of such duty and, if so, in what respects?*

The contract between EDAC and Morgan was formally concluded when Mr Shane orally appointed Morgan architects of International House in May 1969. The terms were not spelled out, but plainly they included those which had applied in previous contracts between Mr Shane's companies and Morgan, since 1955. Clearly Morgan were to design and supervise the construction of a building of the standard which I have described under issue 1, and were to be paid in accordance with the usual Royal Institute of British Architects scale. In the absence of any express agreement I think that the life of International House was to be that which was to be expected of a building of that standard, which I will put at not less than 70 years. During that period it would require maintenance from time to time but not to any substantial parts. "Supervision of construction" would involve acting as "the architect" for the purposes of a standard form of building contract between EDAC and a contractor and would carry with it an obligation to inspect the works as they proceeded.

Morgan's inspections were to be marginally more frequent than those usually made by architects in their position. This is because of Mr Shane's insistence and because he agreed to pay an extra £100 a year as travelling expenses to facilitate inspections.

Nothing was said before or when the contract was made to exclude or restrict the term normally to be implied in contracts for the engagement of architects that Morgan would exercise the skill and care of reasonably competent architects.

Subsequently, on 4 July 1969, Morgan informed Mr Shane and Mr Barker that they had obtained the services of a curtain walling consultant and in the autumn of the same year Mr Shane agreed that sub-contractors, who would inevitably include those for curtain walling, should enter into direct warranties, but on neither occasion was it suggested by anyone that as a result Morgan had ceased to be designers so far as the curtain walling was concerned or that their duty to exercise skill and care should be limited.

In the absence of agreement to the contrary architects cannot escape liability to their clients by delegating their duties to others: Sir Walker Carter, QC, Official Referee, in *Moresk Cleaners Ltd* v *Hicks Ltd* [1966] 2 Ll R 338 at p 343, Judge Sir William Stabb, QC, Official Referee, in *Merton* v *Lowe* (1979) unreported, transcript p 16, and Waller LJ in the Court of Appeal in *Merton* (1981) 18 BLR 130 at p 148.

Morgan's obligation to design International House was not, I think, a once and for all obligation, performed when a complete set of working drawings, which included Alpine's, was sent to Moss. Morgan had both the right and the duty to check their initial design as work proceeded and to correct it if necessary: Napier CJ in the Full Court of South Australia in *Edelman* v *Boehm* [1964] South Australia Law Society Judgment Notices and Sachs LJ in *Brickfield Properties Ltd* v *Newton* [1971] 1 WLR 862 at p 873, applied by Judge Stabb in *Merton* v *Lowe* transcript at p 17 and by me in *Chelmsford* v *Evers* (1983) 25 BLR 99.

I think that Morgan's obligation to design a satisfactory building ended only when International House reached practical completion, which I will take as being the date when Morgan issued a certificate to that effect, namely, on or about 9 June 1977.

Morgan's duty to supervise and inspect must also have continued until practical completion.

Apart from obligations in contract and in the absence of any agreement to the contrary, Morgan plainly owed to EDAC a duty of care in negligence, which was, I think, precisely the same as their duty in contract. Morgan's duty in negligence obviously extended to design and to supervision and inspection and in my view it again, like their obligations in contract, continued until practical completion.

From Morgan's first involvement with International House in 1965 they planned to use curtain walling on its main elevations and they persisted in using it despite Mr Shane's misgivings of 1967. This cannot, I think, be the subject of criticism. Curtain walling has respectable origins in the use of glass and stone in Gothic perpendicular, of glass and iron in the nineteenth century railway sheds and the Crystal Palace and of glass and steel in certain notable inter-war buildings as the Bauhaus and Peter Jones. Since the 1939–45 war aluminium has usually been preferred to steel for window frames because it is more malleable and does not have to be painted. In the 1960s glass and aluminium curtain walling was very fashionable with architects and was widely used. Putty was applied to steel and required regular replacement. Sealants, based on chemicals, was used with aluminium and certainly if protected from rain and from sunlight and were expected to last for 20 or more years without attention.

Modern developments in materials and technologies in the construction industry have been so numerous and so rapid as to exceed the ability of even the most talented and assiduous professional men to master them all. Architects and others must of necessity seek assistance when they reach the limits of their knowledge. Curtain walling may not be particularly difficult for trained architects to understand, but the experts who gave evidence were generally of the opinion that the ordinary competent architect would have had little knowledge of the subject.

I am not certain about the extent of Mr Branch's knowledge of curtain walling, but Mr Rae had, as I have said, both studied curtain walling and been concerned with using it on sites. Nevertheless, they were both aware that they had limitations and, partly perhaps because of Mr Shane's anxieties, but in any event very sensibly, they went to Winmart for help. Morgan employed Winmart to prepare details, and a specification and a revised specification of curtain walling, to recommend companies from whom tenders to become sub-contractors should be obtained, and to advise on the tenders. That was the position when in 1970 further progress with International House was suspended. Up to

that time, in my view, despite a letter from Mr Sulston protesting that
Winmart had not been asked to give drawings, Morgan had exercised
all the skill and care that could be expected of them.

Unfortunately, however, when the scheme was reactivated in 1971
Morgan allowed haste to prevail over care. They did not give Winmart
an opportunity to revise their details and specification before seeking
new tenders, although, even if their reading had not informed them of
DD4 and other developments, they might have guessed that technical
invention had not stood still. They invited a tender from Alpine without making proper enquiries about them or asking Winmart to do so.
Enquiries would have revealed that Alpine had been in business for a
short time only. Morgan failed even to make certain that Alpine
received a copy of Winmart's specification.

On receipt of Alpine's somewhat superficial tender, on which there
was a reference to an alleged similar scheme in Southampton, Mr Rae
failed to investigate properly. If he had done so, he would have
discovered that the use of curtain walling in Southampton was quite
unlike that proposed for Ashford and would surely have had no further
dealings with Alpine. Mr Rae asked for, but failed to obtain, Alpine's
confirmation that their proposals complied with Winmart's specification. Mr Rae brought about three short and I think quite inadequate
meetings attended by Mr Trotman and Mr Plough but no steps were
taken to obtain Winmart's fully considered advice in confidence. They
instructed Moss to accept a tender from Alpine, when neither they
themselves nor Winmart's had approved it. They expected, but did not
ensure, that Alpine and Winmart would co-operate in the preparation
of working drawings.

On Mr Rae receiving Alpine's revised details, he did not instruct
Winmart to check them, but did so himself and, either because of lack
of knowledge or lack of care, passed them, when, on account of their
many weaknesses, he manifestly ought not to have done so. After
receiving Mr Plough's letter of 22 September 1972 Mr Rae and Mr
Branch both knew that Winmart had not checked Alpine's working
drawings, but they nonetheless allowed Alpine to produce the curtain
walling. In October 1972 Mr Rae checked further drawings submitted
to him by Alpine and approved them, when obviously he should not
have done so.

On 17 November 1972 Morgan issued Alpine's drawings to Moss,
thereby finally adopting as their own an initial design which was defective in the many respects which I have mentioned under the third
issue.

On 14 December 1972 Morgan agreed to Lux-Fix installing the
curtain walling without prior consultation with Winmart or Moss and
without enquiring about Lux-Fix. At the very beginning of 1972 an

uninformative water test was carried out, but by that time installation had commenced.

It would undoubtedly have been prudent of Morgan to have employed Winmart to have carried out at least the early supervision and inspection required in respect of the curtain walling on their behalf, but I do not think that they could have been blamed on that account, if they had carried out the inspections and supervision properly themselves. Unfortunately, they did not do so.

I think that neither in respect of Block B nor Block A did Mr Rae make a sufficient effort to know what was going on. If he had, he must have discovered many of the defects in workmanship which were occurring and also the difficulties being encountered applying sealants. He might even have come to realise the deficiencies in the design. I think that Mr Rae's failure was the more regrettable, since as I have said I accept Mr Barker's evidence as to Mr Rae's 1978 description of Lux-Fix's workmen.

Mr Branch's inspections were, I think, as ineffective as those of Mr Rae. As the partner in charge of the project, he should in my view have been much more active. It was most unfortunate that it was not until the installation of the curtain walling was complete that Morgan came to know that it leaked.

On making that discovery Morgan's reactions were to seek, through Moss, Alpine's assurance that the curtain walling was not defective, when it obviously was, and to request Mr Plough to make a single visit, but not to provide him with drawings or any means of examining the curtain walling externally.

Morgan did not exercise their power under condition 6(3) of the head contract to require the opening up of any part of the curtain walling; they did not attempt to investigate what had gone wrong themselves nor did they instruct Winmart or any other consultants to investigate on their behalf.

Instead of grappling with the situation, Morgan simply allowed Alpine to make repeated attempts to stop the leaks by external applications of mastics, without even issuing instructions authorising them under condition 11 of the head contract. I think that Mr Rae, if not Mr Branch, must have known sufficient about sealants to realise that exposed ones could not provide a lasting solution. After the immediate failure of the first attempt they must have realised that even a temporary solution was unlikely to be achieved. Mr Rae and Mr Branch must also have observed the poor standard of workmanship.

I find Morgan's excuse for inactivity, namely fear of prejudicing EDAC's rights against Moss or against Alpine, if they took the initiative and gave specific instructions as to what should be done, very unconvincing. They knew that either Alpine's design or workmanship, or both, were at fault, so that Alpine were in breach of the direct warranty and/or of their sub-contract with Moss. Under the head contract Morgan had powers to give instructions to Moss, which would be passed on to Alpine. Morgan were employed by EDAC to exercise responsibility; instead they simply hoped for the best.

Morgan should have discovered what was wrong with the curtain walling by requiring it to be opened up and by obtaining whatever expert advice they needed. They should then, again with expert help, have prepared a scheme for putting the curtain walling right. That would have required a redesign; making use of existing materials when, if at all, possible. I do not think that removal of all or most of the existing curtain walling and its replacement could have been brought about by instructions given under the head contract, as they would have constituted too great a departure from it. Morgan should have informed EDAC fully of the position and advised what was needed.

I have no doubt that Mr Shane would have accepted advice frankly given; in any event EDAC would have had no alternative but to agree to fundamental changes if they were ever to obtain a satisfactory building. EDAC would, of course, have been put to very considerable expense, but still a good deal less than they are likely now to incur. EDAC would have had the same remedies as at present and Alpine might not have gone into liquidation.

In my opinion Morgan's various acts and omissions after the beginning of 1971, to which I have referred, constituted breaches of duty in contract, because they fell below the standard of skill and care to be expected of reasonably competent architects. For exactly the same reasons I think that they also constituted breaches of duty in negligence.

Still dealing with the fourth issue, questions relating to Moss read:
(b) (i) *Did Moss owe EDAC any duty to warn of design defects at any and, if so, what stage?*
   (ii) *If so, were Moss in breach of such duty and, if so, in what respects?*
(d) (i) *During and after the installation of the curtain walling what duties of inspection and/or supervision and/or investigation and/or calling for an investigation (by themselves and/or others) and which did Moss owe to EDAC?*
   (ii) *Were Moss in breach of any (and, if so, which) such duties and in what respects?*
(e) *Were Moss in breach of any and, if so, which contractual duties in respect of curtain walling defects?*

The head contract between EDAC and Moss contained, *inter alia*, the following conditions, omitting words irrelevant for present purposes:

   "Condition 1(1). The Contractor shall ... carry out and complete the Works shown upon the contract drawings and described . . . in the contract bills . . . to the reasonable satisfaction of the architect.

Condition 1(2). If the contractor shall find any discrepancy in or divergence between the . . . drawings . . . and/or the . . . bills he shall immediately give a written notice . . . and the architect shall issue instructions in regard thereto.

Condition 2(1). The Contractor shall . . . forthwith comply with all instructions issued to him by the architect . . .

Condition 4(1). The Contractor shall comply with, and give all Notices required by . . . any instrument . . . made under any Act of Parliament. . . . The Contractor before making any variations from the Contract drawings or . . . bills necessitated by such compliance shall give to the architect written notice specifying the reason for such variation and the architect may issue instructions in regard thereto. If within 7 days of having given the said . . . notice the Contractor does not receive any instructions regarding the matters therein specified, he shall proceed with the work conforming to the . . . instrument . . . in question and any variation thereby necessitated shall be deemed to be a variation required by the architect.

Condition 6(1). All materials, goods and workmanship shall . . . be of the . . . kinds and standards described in the . . . bills.

Condition 8. The Contractor shall constantly keep upon the works a competent foreman . . .

[and] Condition 27. The following provisions of this condition shall apply when prime cost sums . . . arise as a result of architect's instructions given in regard to the expenditure of provisional sums in respect of persons to be nominated by the architect to supply and fix materials or goods or to execute work. (A) . . . All specialists or others who are nominated by the architect are hereby declared to be sub-Contractors . . . Provided that the architect shall not nominate any persons as sub-Contractor against whom the Contractor shall make reasonable objection, or . . . who will not enter into a sub-Contract which provides . . . (i) that the nominated sub-Contractor shall carry out and complete the sub-Contract works in every respect to the reasonable satisfaction of the Contractor and of the architect . . . (iii) That the nominated sub-Contractor shall indemnify the Contractor against the same liabilities in respect of sub-Contract works as those for which the Contractor is liable to indemnify the employer under this Contract".

In addition condition 28 enabled the architect to nominate suppliers of "materials and goods to be fixed by the Contractor". The condition did not give the contractor any right of objection to a supplier and required only that the materials or goods should be to the satisfaction of the architect. Condition 35 provided for arbitration in respect of disputes, but also that subject to exceptions, which did not include any reference to condition 4, arbitration should not open until after practical completion of the works.

The contract did not contain an express condition requiring the contractor, Moss, to warn the architect, Morgan, or the employers EDAC, of defects in drawings or bills. The contract made no attempt to exclude implied terms.

Apart from obligations in contract, Moss owed normal duties in negligence to those sufficiently proximate to be affected by their acts or omissions, which could certainly include EDAC and so I think Morgan.

Duty to warn. The only English authority relied upon by Mr Desch in support of his contention that Moss owed a duty to warn of design defects was *Duncan* v *Blundell* (1820) 3 Stark 6, in which the plaintiff had by the defendant's order erected a stove in a shop and laid a tube under the floor to carry off smoke, but the plan failed entirely. Bayley J said:

"Where a person is employed in a work of skill, the employer buys both his labour and his judgment; he ought not to undertake the work if he cannot succeed, and he should know whether it will or not; of course it is otherwise if the party employing him choose to supersede the workman's judgement by using his own".

Mr Desch also cited the decision of the Canadian Supreme Court in *Brunswick Construction Limited* v *Nowlan*, (1974) 21 BLR 27, in which an owner had employed an experienced contractor to erect a house for him in accordance with plans prepared by an engineer, but without supervision. The contractor built the house as required by the plans, whereupon dry rot developed in its roof because of lack of ventilation. The Supreme Court held that the contractor had acted in breach of contract. Ritchie J with whom the majority of the court agreed, said at p 34:

"In my opinion a contractor of this experience should recognise the defects in the plans which were so obvious to the architect subsequently employed by the [owner] and knowing of the reliance which was being placed upon it, I think the [contractor] was under duty to warn the [owner] of the danger inherent in executing the plans . . .".

It would seem that both Bayley J's and the Supreme Court's decisions were based upon implied terms.

Whether a term is to be implied in any particular contract depends upon whether it is necessary in order to give to it business efficacy and/or to make it work: *The Moorcock* (1889) 14 PD 64 CA; *Reigate* v *Union Manufacturing Company Ltd* [1918] 1 KB 592 CA; and *Liverpool City Council* v *Irwin* [1977] AC 239. It is not sufficient that a term would have been reasonable; it must have been such that to quote the words of Lord Cross of Chelsea in *Irwin* at p 807:

"If its absence had been pointed out at the time both parties –
assuming them to have been reasonable men – would have agreed
without hesitation to its insertion".

In this case Moss, like the builders in *Duncan* and *Brunswick*, were not
responsible for design. Apart from condition 4(1) their obligations were
simply to carry out the works in accordance with the drawings and bills
and to comply with Morgan's instructions. The possibility of a discrepancy between drawings and bills was recognised but, if Moss found one,
they were not to use their initiative, but only to give notice of the discrepancy.

Unlike the employers in *Duncan* and in *Brunswick*, EDAC had
appointed Morgan to act for them during the carrying out of the works,
instead of relying upon Moss to execute them unsupervised. The works
were, however, very large and costly and Moss were experienced
builders.

I think that if on examining the drawings or as a result of experience on site Moss formed the opinion that in some respect the design
would not work, or would not work satisfactorily, it would have been
absurd for them to have carried on implementing it just the same. In
my view if the directors of EDAC and of Moss had been asked at the
time when the contract was made what Moss should do in those circumstances, they would have agreed at once that Moss should communicate their opinion to Morgan. I think, therefore, that in order to give
efficacy to the contract the term requiring Moss to warn of design
defects as soon as they came to believe that they existed was to be
implied in the contract.

I think that as part of Moss's duty of care in negligence they owed
EDAC and Morgan a duty to inform the latter of design defects known
to them.

Since Moss did not call any witnesses of fact and there was no
direct evidence from any other source as to what their employees did or
did not do, whether Moss came to know of facts which must have led
them to believe that the design was defective has necessarily to be a
matter of inference.

Morgan sent to Moss Alpine's drawings as contract drawings. It
can be readily inferred that an employee or employees of Moss looked
at the drawings. Whether Moss had had much experience of curtain
walling, I do not know. Since, however, Mr Rae, an architect with
experience of curtain walling, spent a day and a half examining the
drawings without detecting defects, I cannot possibly conclude that
they were so obvious that Moss must necessarily have come to know of
them.

Moss was expressly required to keep a general foreman on site. As
might have been expected they had a site agent and other staff at

Ashford and, like Mr Rae and Mr Branch, Moss' staff were present on all working days.

Moss had undertaken the building of International House; an obligation which they performed with their own work force and by sub-contractors. At the very least Moss's staff must I feel certain have seen what was happening on site, including the activities of Lux-Fix's fitters. In my view, because of the amount of curtain walling that had to be fixed, Moss's staff must have become aware of the difficulty of applying sealants in accordance with Alpine's drawings; in other words they must have come to know of the lack of buildability in the design. I think that by failing to warn Morgan of that defect, Moss became in breach of the implied term requiring them to give such warning.

If I am right in inferring that Moss's staff became aware of lack of buildability, then I think that by failing to warn Morgan of it, Moss also acted in breach of duty in negligence.

Liability in respect of nominated sub-contractors. Condition 1(1) required Moss to carry out the contracts works, but condition 27 provided, in a complicated fashion, that Morgan might nominate a person to carry out part of them as a sub-contractor to Moss. The power to nominate was subject to safeguards in favour of Moss, namely, the right to object to the proposed sub-contractor on reasonable grounds and to his willing-ness to enter into a sub-contract with Moss, indemnifying the latter against liability under the head contract. Once the nominated sub-contractor has entered into a sub-contract, there is nothing in the head contract to distinguish him from any other sub-contractor employed by Moss.

Gloucestershire County Council v *Richardson* [1969] 1 AC 480, was a case which arose out of the supply of concrete columns by a sub-contractor employed by a contractor as a result of nomination under the 1939 RIBA contract (with 1957 amendments), which contained conditions identical to 1, 27 and 28 of the present contract. The nomination was under the equivalent of condition 28, but Lord Pearce after quoting words now to be found in condition 27, said at p 495:

"These words seem to make it clear that the contractors accepted liability in respect of work done by the nominated sub-contractor".

Lord Pearson at p 512 said words to the same effect.

Bickerton v *North West Metropolitan Hospital Board* [1970] 1 WLR 607 concerned the 1963 JCT local government form of contract. Lord Reid at p 607 described conditions identical to those of the present head con-tract as "an ingenious method of achieving two objects which at first sight might seem incompatible. The employer wants to choose who is to do the prime cost work and to settle the terms on which it is done and at the same time as to avoid the hazards and difficulties which might arise if he entered into a contract with the person who is chosen to do the work. The scheme creates a chain of responsibility". Lord Dilhorne said at p 623: "I cannot myself see that the extent of the contractor's obligation . . . is in any respect limited or affected by the right of the architect to nominate sub-contractors. He has accepted responsibility for the carrying out and completion of all the contract works, including those to be carried out by the nominated sub-contractor. Once the sub-contractor has been nominated and has entered into the sub-contract, the contractor is as responsible for his work as he is for the works of other sub-contractors employed by him with the leave of the architect."

I think that there can be no doubt that if Alpine were nominated as sub-contractors to supply and fix materials or goods or to execute work, under condition 27, Moss are liable under the head contract in respect of their workmanship, which includes that of Lux-Fix. Moss would also be liable in respect of defects in materials, for example sealants, supplied by Alpine, but none was alleged.

Mr Judge, however, submitted to me that Alpine were not nominated under condition 27, but under condition 28 as suppliers. If that were the position, then, because of the wording of condition 28 and on the authority of the *Gloucestershire County Council* case, Moss would have no responsibility for Alpine. I think there can be no doubt that Alpine were physically to attach the curtain walling to the structure of International House and were to perform other consequential work on site. I think, therefore, that they were suppliers and fixers nominated under condition 27.

Mr Judge further submitted that the existence of the direct warranty agreement between EDAC and Alpine relieved Moss of liability in respect of Alpine's workmanship under the head contract. The direct warranty made no reference to workmanship, but, in any event, the existence of a contract between EDAC and Alpine, to which Moss were not parties and under which they had no rights, could not affect their liability under the head contract.

I conclude that Moss are liable in respect of defects in work carried out by Alpine in performance of Moss's obligation to carry out works pursuant to the head contract. The question has not been argued before me but I am inclined to the view that Moss are not liable for Alpine's bad workmanship in carrying out the remedial measures, since they had not been instructed formally by Morgan under the head contract.

Since Alpine were in relation to Moss independent contractors, there can be no question of Moss being vicariously liable in tort for negligence by Alpine.

Duty to comply with statutory provisions. Condition 4(1) of the head contract is expressed in mandatory terms: "the contractor shall comply with any instrument made under an Act of Parliament . . ." A similar condition in the 1939 RIBA contract came before the Court of Appeal in

Townsends (Builders) Limited v *Cinema News and Property Management Limited* [1958] 20 BLR 118.

In it a builder had agreed to carry out alterations to a house in accordance with plans prepared by an architect. The plans showed two bathroom-lavatories opening into habitable rooms, contrary to the local authority's bye-laws. The builder had not given notice to the authority that he was starting work, as the architect had said that he would do so. The builder did not realise when he started forming the bathroom-lavatories that he was infringing the bye-law, but he continued after he came to know the position. The Court of Appeal held that the builder was liable to the householder, but that the architect should indemnify him because the architect had stated that he would give the notice and the builder had relied upon his statement. Text book writers have suggested that the case was a forerunner of *Hedley Byrne* v *Heller* [1964] AC 465, but I am doubtful whether that is so. In *Hedley Byrne* the defendants made a statement negligently; in *Townsends* the architect had made a promise, apparently without consideration, which he did not keep.

Mr Desch submitted that because of the wording of condition 4(1) and in the light of *Townsends'* case it should be read as imposing liability upon Moss for breach of a statutory provision regardless of whether or not they knew that they were in breach of the provision.

Mr Judge submitted that if Mr Desch's be the correct construction of condition 4(1), it was so inconsistent with condition 1(1), which required Moss to carry out the works in accordance with the plans and bills, that it should be rejected as repugnant to the earlier and main condition.

Mr Judge cited to me the Privy Council case of *Forbes* v *Git* [1922] 1 AC 256, in which in an appeal from Canada, which concerned a building contract, Lord Wrenbury said at p 259:

"The principle of law to be applied may be stated in few words. If in a Deed an earlier clause is followed by a later clause which destroys altogether the obligation caused by the earlier clause, the earlier clause prevails. In this case the two clauses cannot be reconciled and the earlier provision of the Deed prevails over the later."

Unfortunately the question of whether the condition requiring compliance with by-laws was repugnant to other conditions in the contract was not raised in *Townsends'* case, so that the Court of Appeal's decision does not provide any guidance on the point. In my opinion, however, while Moss's obligations under condition 4(1) might on occasions be inconsistent with their obligations under condition 1(1) the inconsistency would be unlikely to be such as would, to adopt Lord Wrenbury's words, "destroy altogether" their obligations under condition 4(1). Moss have in any event, regardless of contract, a duty to comply with statutory requirements. Both conditions 1(1) and 4(1)

have long existed in standard forms of construction contracts. I hold
that condition 4(1) cannot be rejected as repugnant.

In this case the statutory instrument which Moss is alleged to have
infringed is C8 of the Building Regulations, 1972, made under the
Public Health Acts, which reads (omitting irrelevant words):

"Any external wall, including any parapet . . . forming part of an
external wall . . . shall be so constructed so as not to transmit moisture
due to rain or snow to any part of the building which would be adversely
affected by such moisture and . . . shall be so constructed as adequately
to resist the penetration of such moisture to the inside of the building".
Mr Judge questioned whether the curtain walling at International
House came within Regulation C8, but I have no doubt that it does. The
curtain walling and connected parapets formed the exterior of four
elevations of the building. The curtain walling is not weight-bearing,
but the regulation does not require that walls should be. The regulation
does not prescribe the materials of which a wall should be made; there
is no reason, therefore, why one should not have been of glass and
aluminium.

In *Townsends'* case it should have been obvious to the builder that
the new rooms would be contrary to the bye-law. In the present case
Moss were required to carry out works pursuant to a design shown on
drawings and, since Mr Rae, a qualified and experienced architect,
failed to find any defect on examination of the drawings, Moss must be
excused for having failed to do so. Moss only became aware of defects in
the design on discovering its lack of buildability.

To construe condition 4(1) as imposing upon Moss liability for
failing to comply with the regulation at times when reasonably they
were totally unaware of the breach seems decidedly harsh. However,
because of the clear words of condition 4(1) and in view of *Townsends'*
case I have no alternative but to reach that conclusion.

But that is not the end of the matter. Although Moss acted in
breach of condition 4(1) by constructing by their sub-contractor,
Alpine, curtain walling which did not comply with Building Regulation C8, they were at the time acting in accordance with condition 1(1).
It was Alpine's drawings issued by Morgan as architects under the
head contract which caused Moss to act in breach of condition 4(1).

Mr Judge submitted to me that where an act which is not manifestly illegal is done by one person at the request of another and turns
out to be injurious to the rights of a third person, the person doing the
act is entitled to an indemnity against his liability to the third person
from the person who required that the act should be done. In support of
that proposition Mr Judge relied on *Sheffield Corporation* v *Barclay* [1905]
AC 392, *The Secretary of State* v *Bank of India Limited* [1938] 2 All ER 797 PC
and *Yeung Kai Yung* v *Hong Kong Banking* [1981] AC 787 PC, all of which

were concerned with financial transactions, and also upon *Townsends'* case. Mr Judge claimed that Moss were entitled to be indemnified by Morgan against EDAC's claim for breach of condition 4(1).

I think that that up to the time when Moss must have discovered the lack of buildability in aspects of the design of curtain walling, Moss probably would be entitled to an indemnity from Morgan if found liable to EDAC. However, Morgan were, as architects under the head contract, EDAC's agents: therefore Moss would equally well be entitled to indemnity from EDAC. In the circumstances it seems to me that the doctrine of circuity must apply to defeat EDAC's claim. A plea of circuity of action has been recognised in recent years in actions in negligence and for breach of statutory duty, see *Ginty* v *Belmont Building Supplies Ltd* [1959] 1 All ER 414 and *Post Office* v *Hampshire County Council* [1980] 1 QB 124 CA, but if I understand aright the pre-1975 precedent in Bullen & Leake's *Pleading and Practice*, they indicate that it can apply generally.

My conclusion is that initially Moss were not liable for breach of condition 4(1), but that once they became aware of defects in design which necessarily involved a breach of the regulation, they should have given notice of it in accordance with the condition and, since they did not do so, they became in breach of contract, in respect of which, since the failure was their own, they cannot claim indemnity or shelter behind circuity of action. Their obligation was in substance the same as their duty to warn of design defects under an implied term in the contract and in negligence.

Duty to inspect. Since Moss had undertaken to carry out works in accordance with the contract plans and bills and since, as I have held, they were potentially liable in respect of all sub-contractors' work they had an obvious personal interest in inspecting, supervising and, if necessary, investigating by themselves or by others the installation of the curtain walling and other work undertaken by sub-contractors.

Because Moss themselves had such strong reasons for inspecting and the like, it does not follow that they owed duties to do so to anyone else. The contract expressly required them to keep a competent foreman on the site, but did not expressly require that he should do anything!

I think, however, that Moss by entering into the head contract and undertaking to build International House became managers of the site with overall charge of work upon it. I conclude that yet another term must be implied in the contract in order to give it efficacy, namely, one requiring that Moss inspect and supervise work by their own employees and by sub-contractors, whether nominated or otherwise. I think that Moss owed a similar duty to EDAC to inspect and to supervise in negligence. On the assumption that investigation means more than inspection and supervision, in my view there is no duty in contract or negligence for Moss to carry it out. What Moss had to do was to ensure that work was done according to the plans and bills. If any investigation was required, for example, by water tests upon curtain walling, that was a task for Morgan.

Just as Mr Rae should, as I have held, have discovered Lux-Fix's bad workmanship and also their real difficulty in applying sealants in accordance with the drawings, so I think that Moss's site agent, foreman and other staff should have done so. Moss's staff had greater opportunities than Mr Rae because they were on site all the time. They either failed to inspect and to supervise or did not do so competently.

Moss's own bad workmanship. Moss's employees built the parapets; they failed to place the damp proof courses correctly and seal the weep holes. Moss's workmen also failed in places to provide vertical damp proof courses at the corners. Moss are personally liable in respect of their own bad workmanship.

The next questions under issue 4 concern Winmart and read:

(f) (i) *What duties did Winmart owe to EDAC?*

(ii) *In what respects (if any) were they in breach thereof?*

(g) (i) *What duties did Winmart owe to Morgan?*

(ii) *In what respects (if any) were they in breach thereof?*

There was no contract between EDAC and Winmart, but only between Morgan and Winmart. In that contract there was, I think, a term requiring that Winmart should exercise the skill and care to be expected of competent curtain walling consultants. I think that Winmart must have owed duties in negligence to both Morgan and EDAC. The standard of care required of them in negligence was broadly the same as that in contract.

The duties which Winmart owed had to be performed within the general scope of their employment by Morgan. They could and I think did on occasions draw attention to the need for further work to be done to avoid risks, but they could not officiously advise or inspect when not asked to do so. They could therefore only be blamed if they failed to perform correctly what their instructions allowed them to do.

I have already commented upon the manner in which Morgan used Winmart. Up to 1969 Winmart were employed appropriately. On occasions in 1972 and subsequent years Winmart were instructed by Morgan, but were in my view never given proper opportunities and facilities to provide their services efficiently.

I think that it would have been better for everyone if after 1971 Winmart had refused to act for Morgan altogether, instead of from time to time protesting at not being employed properly and then falling in with Morgan's wishes once again. Winmart cannot, however, be accused of having gone along with Morgan's requests from grasping motives, for their fees were always very modest.

I think that up to 1969 Winmart did their work efficiently, but from 1972 they did the best they could in the circumstances. I think that they came nearest to having acted in breach of duty on the occasion of the water test in January 1973. Mr Plough was not present on that occasion and Mr Perry did not point out the limited usefulness of the test. Once again, however, Winmart may, I think, shelter behind their lack of full instructions.

I conclude that Winmart have not acted in breach of duty to Morgan nor to EDAC.

The last group of questions under issue 4 are in respect of Alpine:
(i) *What (if any) duties did Alpine owe to:*
    (a) *EDAC*
    (b) *Moss*
    (c) *Morgan*
in respect of:
(i) *Design, and*
(ii) *Supply and/or erection and/or installation?*
(ii) *If so, were Alpine in breach of such duties and, if so, in what respects?*
Alpine by admitting liability and not being present at all during this sub-trial have, in substance, agreed to my answering these questions adversely to them, and my answers can therefore be very brief.

I think that Alpine owed duties in contract to EDAC under the direct warranty and to Moss under the sub-contract between them and in tort to EDAC, Moss and Morgan. Alpine's contractual duty to EDAC related to design and materials and their contractual duty to Moss and Morgan related to design, materials and workmanship.

Alpine acted in breach of its design duties by providing a thoroughly defective initial design and their numerous remedial measures were also defective in design. Alpine, Lux-Fix and Alpine's later sub-contractors provided bad workmanship at all material stages. Among Alpine's many faults was a failure to supervise Lux-Fix properly.

Issue 6 reads:
(6) *To what extent did any breaches of duty by any defendant cause damage to EDAC (the court reserving all questions of quantum both in principle and as to amount for later determination)?*
In respect of breaches of contract my attention was drawn to *Heskell v Continental Express* [1950] 1 All ER 1033 in which Devlin J (as he then was) said at p 1048:
    ". . . I am satisfied that if a breach of contract is one of two causes, both co-operating and both of equal efficacy . . . is sufficient to carry judgment for damages".

I was also referred to *Carslogie Steamship Company Limited* v *Royal Norwegian Government* [1952] AC 292, *Performance Cars* v *Abraham* [1962] 1 QB 33 CA, *Barnett* v *Chelsea Hospital* [1969] 1 QB 426, (Nield J) *Cutler* v *Vauxhall* [1971] 1 QB 418 CA and *Bury* v *Stone & Manganese* [1972] unreported (Ashworth, J) in each of which the questions arose of whether the consquences of a negligent act were subsumed in damage resulting from other causes, such as weather or the results of another negligent act.

Taking breaches of contract first: Alpine's breach of the direct warranty as to design and Morgan's breach of contract to design, each of which obligations continued until practical completion of International House, have resulted in EDAC having a buiding which has leaked more or less continuously to date and curtain walling all or most of which will have to be removed and replaced by new curtain walling of different design at very considerable cost.

Morgan's breaches of contract to inspect and supervise the work resulted in Morgan failing to discover and to stop bad workmanship, which resulted in greater leaks than would otherwise had occurred. Since EDAC had not been in personal occupation of International House, to what extent additional leaks have caused monetary or other loss, I do not at present know.

Moss's breaches of contract in failing on discovering lack of buildability in the design to give warning of it and at the same time to give written notice of breach of the Building Regulations to Morgan, meant that the latter did not even receive warnings which should have concentrated their minds and so brought about redesign, but whether it would have done so is not certain. For the avoidance of doubt, I do not think that Moss's liability can extend to replacement of the curtain walling.

Moss's breaches of contract by reason of bad workmanship for which their sub-contractor Alpine was responsible resulted in more leaks than would otherwise have occurred, but the extent to which that affected EDAC personally I do not know. Moss had no liability in relation to the remedial works attempted by Alpine. Moss's breaches of contract in failing to inspect and supervise their own and sub-contractors' work once again led to additional leaks, with the same consequences for EDAC about which I am uncertain.

Moss's breaches of contract by creating parapet walls which permit leaks into the the curtain walling make it necessary for EDAC to take down all or some of the walls and to rebuild them. The walls would have required remedying even if not linked with the curtain walling. The lack of damp proof course in the vertical abutments will also have to be remedied.

Turning to negligence: Alpine's breaches of duty in relation to design and workmanship have the same consequences for EDAC as those which I have mentioned in connection with their branches of contract.

Morgan's breaches of duty and negligence in respect of design and inspection and supervision have the same results as their breaches of contract.

Moss's negligence in failing to warn of lack of buildability and to inspect and supervise have the same uncertain consequences as had their parallel breaches of contract.

Issue 7 reads:

In the premises:

(a) *Are Moss and/or Alpine and/or Morgan jointly and/or severally liable to EDAC in respect of curtain walling defects?*

(b) *If jointly, in what proportion is each liable?*

(c) *What rights of contribution and/or indemnity arise between the defendants inter se?*

Alpine, Morgan and Moss are each separately liable to EDAC in respect of their breaches of contract. The fact that the breaches operated at the same time will not prevent EDAC from recovering from particular defendants against whom EDAC decides to enforce its judgment, all the damages flowing from those defendants' breaches, but EDAC cannot, of course, recover twice over.

Alpine, Morgan and Moss are jointly and severally liable to EDAC in negligence, but again EDAC may enforce their judgment fully against any one of them.

The Law Reform (Married Women & Tortfeasors) Act 1935 did not provide for contribution between contract-breakers, but only, by section 6, between tortfeasors. Moss would, however, be entitled to recover any sums which they had to pay to EDAC under the head contract on account of Alpine's bad workmanship from Alpine under the sub-contract between them.

Under section 6 of the 1935 Act contribution may be recovered between tortfeasors as may be found by the court "to be just and equitable having regard to the extent of that person's responsibility for the damage".

I think that in relation to liablity in negligence for the defective design and so for replacement of the curtain walling, a just and equitable apportionment would be:

Alpine   75 per cent
Morgan   25 per cent

In relation to negligence resulting in bad workmanship in the curtain walling (as opposed to the parapet walling and vertical damp proof courses) causing whatever loss EDAC may have sustained due to additional leaks, I think that the apportionment should be:

Alpine   80 per cent
Morgan   5 per cent
Moss   15 per cent

For the avoidance of doubt Moss alone should bear all the liability in relation to the parapet walls and vertical damp proof courses.

Issue 8 is:

Are any of EDAC's causes of action against Moss or Morgan statute-barred and to what extent?

Dates which were six years before the issue of EDAC's writ and two amendments to their statement of claim against Morgan were 12 May 1974, 25 February 1977 and 22 April 1977 respectively. The date of practical completion was 9 June 1977.

As I have already said under issue 4 (questions relating to Morgan) Morgan's obligation to design, which included checking their initial design and redesigning if necessary, was continuous. It ended only at practical completion, when, if they had excercised proper skill and care, EDAC would have had a building of the correct standard.

Morgan's obligations to supervise and to inspect, including opening up and the like, also continued until practical completion. If they had been carried out efficiently, not only would the need for further consideration of design have been realised earlier, but some bad workmanship corrected and others stopped.

I think that the reference to design in the original statement of claim was by itself wide enough to include redesign, but in any event six years before the first amendment which referred expressly to redesign was before practical completion. In my view EDAC's claims in respect of defective design, including redesign, both in contract and in negligence, are not statute-barred.

Where in the case of continuing breach of duty some loss was sustained by a plaintiff outside the limitation period and some within, the court must attempt to distinguish between them: *Bury* v *Stone & Manganese* (1972) mentioned previously. The burden of proving that a plaintiff's claim is statute-barred is obviously on he that asserts that it is, namely, the defendant.

In this case I am uncertain whether any loss sustained by EDAC because of Morgan's failure to supervise and inspect properly should be regarded as having accrued outside the limitation period. It follows, I think, that Morgan have not discharged the relevant burden of proof and that EDAC's claim under this head is not statute-barred.

Moss do not assert that EDAC's claims against them are statute-barred.

Issue 9 is:

In the event of any breach of duty being established against any party at what date does the breach occur and what consequences arose from such breach or breaches?

I think that in dealing with previous issues I have already provided answers as precisely as I can to the questions posed in this issue, and that nothing will be gained by repetition.

In conclusion my judgment concerning liability is that:

Alpine are liable to EDAC for breach of the warranty agreement and in negligence for defective design and workmanship.

Alpine is liable to Moss under the sub-contract between them for bad workmanship.

Morgan are liable to EDAC for breach of contract and negligence in respect of defective design, inspection and supervision.

Moss are liable to EDAC for breach of the head contract and negligence in failing to warn of the design's lack of buildability, in failing to give notice of breach of the Building Regulations when they came to know of it, in failing to inspect and supervise Alpine's and Alpine's sub-contractors' work and in respect of their own bad workmanship in connection with the walls and flank elevations. Moss are also liable to EDAC in contract in respect of Alpine's and Alpine's sub-contractors' initial bad workmanship, but not in relation to remedial work.

COUNSEL

For EDAC: Mr Stephen Desch QC and Mr R. Gaitskell (instructed by Rowe & Maw).

For William Moss: Mr Igor Judge QC and Mr N. Baker (instructed by Moss Toone & Deane).

For Winmart: Mr A. Moses (instructed by Davies Arnold & Cooper).

For Morgan Branch: Mr M. Collins QC and Mr A. White (instructed by Payne Hicks Beach & Co).

Architect's duty to warn clients before using untried or little tried materials – Contractor's duty to warn architect of defects of design – Meaning of "latent" damage – Contributory negligence as defence to claim in contract – Circuity of action as a defence – Liability of architects to contractors in tort – Liability of sub-contractors to contractors in tort.

VICTORIA UNIVERSITY OF MANCHESTER	Plaintiffs
v	
HUGH WILSON & LEWIS WOMERSLEY (a firm) AND POCHIN (CONTRACTORS) LTD	Defendants

Queen's Bench Division
(Official Referees' Business)
24, 25, 26 January 1984; 1, 2, 8, 9, 13, 14, 15,
16, 20, 21, 22, 23 February; 3, 4, 5, 9, 10, 14
(view), 16, 17, 18 April; 1, 2, 3, 4, 9, 10, 15 May
and 15 October 1984.

His Honour Judge
John Newey QC

Liability of architects and contractors in relation to design considered.

This action arose out of a major development for the plaintiffs known as the Precinct Centre, erected in two phases between 1968 and 1976. The first defendants were the architects for the development; the second defendants the main contractors and the third defendants nominated sub-contractors. The architects' design called for a building of reinforced concrete (which was not waterproof) to be clad partly in red Accrington bricks and partly in ceramic tiles. In due course many of the tiles fell off and the University adopted a remedial plan which involved the erection of brick cladding with a cavity between bricks and tiles and with the brick walls attached to the structure by steel ties.

On the fifth day of the trial the plaintiffs and the first defendants reached a settlement. Before the trial the third defendants had gone into liquidation and were not represented. Although the trial continued effectively as an action against the contractors, the learned judge decided that it was necessary also to consider the responsibility of the architects and sub-contractors.

HELD: (1) It was not wrong in itself to use the relatively untried method of cladding with ceramic tiles but it did call for special caution. The architects should have warned the plaintiffs of the dangers inherent in using a new method. The architects' design was defective in many respects. In particular it failed to protect the tiles from rain and gave insufficient attention to the building problems of fixing the tiles. Further, the architects had not adequately inspected the fixing.

(2) The defects in fixing the tiles were so extensive that they should have been discovered by the clerk of works.

(3) The contractors were under a duty by virtue of an implied term of their contract with the plaintiffs to warn of any defects in design which they believed to exist but in the circumstances they were not in breach of this duty.

(4) Although the architects had never issued a final certificate in respect of either phase I or phase II, retention money had been released to the sub-contractors against an indemnity given by them to the contractors against latent defects. A latent defect is one which would not be discovered by such an examination as a reasonably careful man skilled in that matter would make; *Charles Brown & Co* v *Nitrate Producers' Steamship Company* [1937] 58 Lloyds Rep 188 applied. Accordingly the defects in fixing by the sub-contractors were not latent defects so as to give rise to an indemnity as between contractor and sub-contractor. However, as between plaintiff and contractor, JCT 1963 condition 27 (e) only protected the contractor in respect of the sub-contractors' failings and not in respect of his own failure adequately to supervise.

(5) The sub-contractors failed adequately to fix the tiles.

(6) The contributory negligence of the architect and/or the clerk of works was no defence to the plaintiffs' claim against the contractors in contract.

(7) In the circumstances the contractors could not rely on a defence of circuity of actions.

(8) The proper measure of damage in the plaintiffs' claim against the contractors was the cost of retiling the building in 1980. It was immaterial that the building would never be retiled because the plaintiffs had (properly) adopted a more expensive remedial solution. It was also immaterial that the plaintiffs had in principle a claim for the same loss against the architects. However, the contractors were not liable for the loss which arose out of the architects' initial design decision to use tiles.

(9) In certain circumstances an architect may owe a duty of care to a contractor. However, the architects did not owe the contractors a duty of care in relation to the inspection of the sub-contractors' work.

(10) The sub-contractors owed the contractors a duty in tort as well as in contract to fix the tiles properly.

HIS HONOUR JUDGE JOHN NEWEY QC: In this consolidated action the plaintiffs are the Victoria University of Manchester (the University) and the defendants are respectively Hugh Wilson and Lewis Womersley (the architects), Pochin (Contractors) Ltd (the contractors) and Hulme & Potts Ltd (the sub-contractors).

The action concerns a large group of buildings known as the Precinct Centre, situated at the northern end of the Manchester Educational Precinct, adjacent to Booth Street, and straddling Oxford Road, which passes approximately north-south through the precinct.

The precinct is about a thousand yards long and at its southern end is the Whitworth Art Gallery, made of red brick of varying sizes, so that many of the bricks look as if they were tiles. Despite the presence of several large concrete faced buildings and of a stone church, the majority of buildings within the precinct, including the original university building designed by Alfred Waterhouse, are of red brick.

In 1963 the University, Manchester City Council and other bodies with interests in the precinct, jointly instructed the architects, who are also town planners, to prepare an overall plan for its development. The architects produced a plan, which recommended the use of red brick and of matching materials on the exteriors of all new buildings and suggested the erection of a "key building" at the precinct's northern end. This last suggestion resulted in the University causing the Precinct Centre to be built primarily as a commercial venture and using private funds and not moneys provided by the University Grants Committee.

Construction was in two phases. During the first there were erected on the west side of Oxford Road show-rooms, stores, a boiler-room and ancillary accommodation at ground and first levels and a shopping arcade at the third level, with above them on the north side students' accommodation, known as Cornford House, up to 11th level, and on the south side office accommodation, called Devonshire House, up to 6th level. There was also built a bridge over Oxford Road at third level, forming an extension to the arcade, and a long pedestrian ramp leading from the footpath on the west side of Oxford Road to the arcade.

During the second phase buildings were erected on the east side of Oxford Road, with an open court in their midst, and including a service area and a car park at ground level and offices at first and second levels, with on the north side offices, called Crawford House, up to 8th level.

The Precinct Centre was connected at its western side to the University's Ecumenical Centre and on its eastern side to the Manchester Business School, itself completed in 1970.

The architects were employed as such throughout; the contractors were employed for both phases, but under separate JCT private edition (with quantities) Contracts (1967 and 1969 revisions respectively), the sub-contractors were nominated as such under each contract but entered into a direct warranty agreement with the University only in respect of phase II; and the same companies were nominated, again under each contract, to fix balustrades and lightning conductors.

The structure of the buildings was of reinforced concrete, which was not waterproof. Except for two glazed areas over parts of the Arcade, all roofs were flat with parapet walls around them. Window details were the same throughout. No concrete was left exposed externally; parts of walls were clad with red Accrington bricks and other parts with red ceramic tiles. Parapet walls had tiled copings and tiles on both sides, with those on the inside carried over upturns from asphalt on the roofs. There were no damp-proof courses in the parapet walls. Soffits, a gutter on the bridge and columns were tiled. The buildings were without protruding features, which would have helped throw water clear of their walls.

No doubt the Centre made an impressive northern entrance to the educational precinct and the colour of the tiles and bricks upon its buildings was fully in accordance with the overall plan for the precinct. Columns on the Business School which were fair faced and waterproof and which its architects, Messrs Cruickshank & Seward, had intended to leave unclad, were tiled, so that they matched the centre. Unhappily the appearance and the resistance to weather of the centre gradually became marred because of tiles failing to adhere to the structure.

On 4 February 1980 the University issued a writ alleging against the architects "breach of duty and/or negligence" and against the contractors "breach of contract and/or negligence and/or breach of statutory duty". At the end of January 1981 the University served the writ, accompanied by a statement of claim. On 1 November 1983 the University amended their statement of claim.

The University pleaded against the architects: that they entered into engagements in respect of phase I in 1966 and in respect of phase II in 1970 and that it was a term of those engagements that they would design and supervise with reasonable care and that the materials used would be reasonably fit for purpose; that they owed to the University a duty of care in negligence; and that in breach of their respective duties, they did not control and supervise properly and designed negligently, so that the tile failures resulted. The University alleged that, if the tile failures occurred before 4 February 1974 the architects were thereafter negligent in failing to ascertain their nature and extent, in not requiring the contractors to carry out remedial work but releasing retention monies in 1976 and in failing to advise as to steps to be taken. They claimed as damages the costs of recladding the building.

The University pleaded against the contractors: that by contracts made under seal on 27 August 1968 and on 8 April 1971 they agreed to construct phases I and II respectively; that they became bound by various express and implied terms in the contracts; that they owed to the University a duty of care in negligence; and that by reason of their negligence and various breaches of contract the tiles failed. The University claimed from the contractors the same damages as they claimed from the architects.

The architects delivered a defence on 3 July 1981 which they amended on 29 November 1983. While admitting some facts alleged by the University as giving rise to breaches of duty, the architects denied any breaches, blamed the contractors and sub-contractors, pleaded contributory negligence and claimed that, if there were a cause of action against them, it was barred by the Limitation Act.

The contractors served a defence on 9 April 1981 and amended it on 7 December 1983. They denied liability, took various points on the wording of the contracts, blamed the architects and sub-contractors and put in issue the amounts claimed. The University delivered replies to both defences.

On 15 October 1982 the contractors served a notice upon the architects under order 16, rule 8, claiming an indemnity against or contribution towards any liability which they might be held to be under to the University, pursuant to the Law Reform (Married Women and Tortfeasors) Act 1935. On 7 December 1983 the contractors amended their notice claiming damages from the architects as an alternative to contribution or indemnity. The Architects also served a contribution notice on the contractors. The contractors' allegations against the architects were based on the University's allegations against the architects. The architects filed a defence to the notice denying liability, repeating their defence to the University and pleading the Limitation Act.

Both the architects and the contractors served third party proceedings on the sub-contractors and on 1 October 1981 the University issued a writ against them and by a subsequent statement of claim, once amended, claimed as damages for negligence in carrying out their work the same damages as they claimed from the other defendants. In defences to all claims against them the sub-contractors denied negligence and also relied upon a limitation defence. Before the commencement of the trial of this action the sub-contractors went into liquidation and at the trial they were not represented.

I have briefly summarised the pleadings exchanged before the trial began, but on its fifth day there was an event which led to radical changes in them. The event was that the University and the architects reached a settlement, a copy of which was subsequently disclosed. I think that the settlement agreement could give rise to problems of construction, but no doubt its overall intention was that:

(1) There should be judgement for the architects against the University;

(2) The University should pursue their claim against the contractors, but would not have to pay the costs of doing so;

(3) In the event of the University receiving less than £1.3m. from the contractors in respect of damages, interest and costs, the architects would pay to them such sums as would increase their recovery to £1.3m;

(4) In the event of the contractors obtaining sums "by way of contribution" from the architects, the University would indemnify them, provided that the University still recovered £1.3m; and

(5) The architects should pay to the University interest on £1.3m. from the date of the agreement or until the University receives £1.3m. at 1 per cent above National Westminster Bank rate from time to time.

Pursuant to the agreement, the University submitted to judgment in favour of the architects and with leave they re-amended their statement of claim in the first action, so as *inter alia* to delete allegations of breaches of clause 4(1) of the contracts, but to add allegations of breaches of implied terms to warn of defects in design and to inspect and supervise sub-contractors' work and to delete completely all allegations of negligence and breaches of statutory duty.

The contractors re-amended their defence by seeking to rely on clause 27(e) of the contracts, answering the University's new allegations specifically, alleging contributory negligence on the part of the University by the architects and by the University's clerk of works, Mr Roper, and – somewhat by way of anticlimax – claiming to set off £1 178 uncertified and unpaid in respect of phase II.

The University's deletion of its allegations of negligence against the contractors had the effect of making it impossible for them to obtain contributions from the architects as joint tortfeasors under s 6(1)(c) of the Act of 1935, but it did not prevent them from pursuing their claim for damages for negligence from them.

After the settlement between the University and the architects, they became allies against the contractors.

Mr Brian Knight and Mr Richard Wilmot-Smith for the University called 15 witnesses. Among them were Dr Beswick, the bursar; Mr Thomas and Mr Crosby, who as planning officers to the University were successively in charge of the University's building programme; Mr Daggett responsible for the Precinct Centre after 1975; Mr Roper, clerk of works employed continuously at the Centre by the University until 1971 and then by the architects; Mr Gibbon of Cruickshank & Seward, the architects responsible for remedial works to the Centre, Mr Seward of Michael Seward and Partners, quantity surveyors for the remedial works; Mr Wear, assistant director of building services; and Mr Crocker of Alan Crocker Associates, independent expert.

Mr Patrick Garland and Mr Christopher Thomas for the contractors called 5 witnesses, namely; Mr Pochin, a director, responsible for phases I and II; Mr Booth, site agent for phase I and contracts manager for phase II; Mr Threlfall of Ove Arup & Partners, structural consultants on phase II; Mr Roberts, a director and quantity surveyor; and Mr Kinnear of Sandbergs, independent expert; Mr Michael Wright and Mr Roger Ter Haar for the architects did not call any witnesses. I did not, therfore, see or hear the architects, nor of course, any representative of the sub-contractors.

I think that all the witnesses did their best to give me truthful accounts of events as they remembered them, but that does not mean that they were always completely right, for many were speaking of what happened 12 to 17 years ago. Among many excellent witnesses of fact I was particularly impressed by Mr Crosby, Mr Daggett, Mr Gibbon and Mr Pochin.

Fortunately for me there was substantial agreement between Mr Crocker and Mr Kinnear. I found their reports, their illustrative sketches and their evidence extremely helpful.

The documentary evidence consisting of contracts, correspondence, minutes and literature extended to more than 4 000 pages. There were also plans and a large number of photographs, which illustrated individual defects and the progressive failure of the tiles. At the request of the parties I visited the Centre on 7 January 1983, when I knew very little about the case, and I visited it again on 14 April 1984, immediately before final speeches. On each occasion I was accompanied by represenatives of the parties.

I will first summarise my findings with regard to the selection, fixing and failure of the tiles and the remedial works and their costs. My summary will be chronological. I shall not refer in detail to the photographs, although I have had them well in mind throughout. I shall summarise Mr Crocker's first report because its date as well as the advice given to the University is significant, but otherwise I shall in the main give effect to the experts' opinions in my conclusions, rather than refer to them in detail, I will state my conclusions under issues, which I will take one by one.

On 14 December 1966 the University appointed the architects under the Standard RIBA conditions to be project architects for the Centre and they, principally by their Mr Armstrong and Mr Wright, began to prepare the specification for phase I. It would appear that the then more senior and experienced members of the firm were not closely involved, which was I think a pity.

The University did not at the time state expressly how long they expected the new Centre to last, but, since it was being built as part of the University Precinct, I think that, despite its largely commercial character, everyone must have understood that the University expected it to have a long life – a hundred years or more. Mr Thomas said that the University wanted trouble-free buildings; by that he did not, of course, mean that maintenance would not be required from time to time, but that no major works would be needed for a long period.

Ceramic tiles had for many centuries been used externally in the Middle East, where they were not subjected to persistent rainfall and any problems caused by changes in temperature were overcome by the use of very thin adhesives. In the 1960s tiles began for the first time to be used on the outsides of buildings in this country. Red tiles with Accrington bricks were used on the prestigious History Library at Cambridge, where they appeared to be successful at first and only failed later. The architects went to see the new library.

In June 1967 the Architects told Mr Thomas during discussions that they were going to propose the use of tiles on the Centre. Mr Thomas, who is an architect, and like most architects had had no experience of tiling, became alarmed. He asked whether the architects knew what they were doing and they assured him that they did.

In fact the architects had never used ceramic tiles externally before. They therefore invited representatives of Building Adhesives Ltd (BAL) and of Geoffrey Woolliscroft & Sons Ltd (Woolliscroft) to call on them and they sought the advice of the British Ceramic Research Association (the Research Association).

On 4 August 1967 BAL wrote to the architects confirming that they had advised the use of Wooliscroft's $6 \times 3 \times 3/8$ in quarry tiles and saying that if the concrete were sufficiently true, which they said was unlikely, the tiles could be fixed with a thin-bed adhesive, CTF2. If a true enough surface were not achieved the concrete could be rendered up and the CTF2 then used; alternatively, the tiles could be fixed direct on to the surface using a thick-bed adhesive, such as Bal-mix or Bal-flex. For filling between the joints Bal-grout might be used, or, if a completely water-proof grouting were required, an epoxy based one.

On 7 August 1967 the Research Association wrote recommending Woolliscroft tiles. They stated that if concrete were flat to a tolerance of plus or minus $1/8$ in screeds could be avoided, but that otherwise a cement-sand mix should be used, that adhesive would have to be applied in a solid bed normally achieved by "buttering" (by which they meant an even application over the whole of the backs of the tiles), that spacer pegs were necessary to provide minimum joints of $1/12$ in and that if joints were grouted with a cement based grout white stains were certain to occur at first and that an epoxy-based grout would be more expensive but waterproof. The Research Establishment stated that expansion joints ¼ in wide would be adequate at floor levels at panel widths of 17 ft 6 in and that the appropriate recommendations of BSCP 212: 1966 Part II should be observed.

CP212 Part II had been published by the General Council for Codes of Practice at the British Standards Institution on 27 June 1966. In its foreword it referred to "Lack of long-term experience in the use of some types of bedding materials with the range of tiles . . . now available". In paragraph 1.2 it defined a thin bedding coat as not in excess of ⅛ in thick and a thick bedding coat as in excess of ⅛ in, which should generally be a ¼ in thick for tiles up to 6 × 6 in.

In paragraph 3.2. it warned that the durability of tiling is dependent upon various factors, including:

"3.2.1.3. The method of fixing the tile . . . its adhesive powers and resistance to water, the effects of frost (and) solar heat"; "3.2.14 grouting . . . the thoroughness of the operation and the composition of the jointing material affect the resistance of the joints between the tiles . . . to water penetration (and) to frost action – a water-proofing agent should be incorporated in the pointing compound . . ." and "3.2.15. tiling on southern exposures is likely to be affected by excessive thermal expansion and may have its adhesion impaired or may develop cracks and bulges – areas of dark coloured tiles absorb solar heat readily and should therefore be kept to a minimum – where it is suspected that thermal movement of tiling may be excessive an adequate width of joint should be provided around each tile to accommodate this movement".

BSCP 212 continued at 3.3.1.

". . . because the tile surface is impermeable water falling on the tiling is concentrated on the joints between the tiles and may penetrate them if the . . . grout is permeable, incomplete or there are cracks . . . The water may enter the tile body, the tile fixing medium and the background and cause loss of adhesion or enable frost action to develop . . .".

Paragraph 3.4.1. recommended that:

"consideration should be given to the use of architectural details . . . for example, advantage may be taken of special features introduced to afford protection for tiling particularly at positions where it is most vulnerable to the penetration of moisture".

Paragraph 3.4.2. warned that:

"parapet walls with tile finishes are a potential source of weakness and require very careful treatments as defects frequently occur in parapets. A parapet wall should be protected by a coping with a damp-proof course immediately beneath it".

Paragraph 3.5. dealt with movement joints:

"3.5.1. experience indicates that compressive stresses are set up in the tiling . . . as a result of movement due to variations in strength and drying shrinkage and background; these stresses can also be caused by the vertical settlement of tiling . . . on a building face. . . . Consideration should therefore be given to the provision of movement joints. These joints which should not be confused with structural expansion joints should extend the depth of the tile bed and should be a minimum of ¼ in wide."

"3.5.2. The designer should detail the disposition of movement joints according to the materials of construction and types of tiles . . . used. These joints will normally be at storey height, horizontally, and approximately 10 ft apart vertically. Ideally, they should coincide with structural material changes . . .".

Paragraph 3.9. referred to

"backgrounds" "3.9.1 The nature of the background to which the tiles are applied is of the utmost importance". "Mechanical key is offered by the nature of the background or is artificially provided". "Trueness of construction is important because of its effect on the thickness of the floated coat, the choice of fixing method and the final appearance of the tiling."

Paragraph 3.10.1. mentioned the importance of ensuring that

"before applying a floated coat sufficient time has elapsed to enable initial drying shrinkage of the background to take place" and also the use of "fixed metal lathing or wire netting" with a weaker background.

Paragraph 3.11.1. related to

"the floated coat" or rendering, of which the purpose "is to form a surface suitable for the application of tiling when the background is unsuitable for the direct fixing of tiling".

3.11.3 stated that

"If the thickness (of the rendering) needed is greater than ½ in it should be built up in two or more coats, each coat not more than ¾ in thick".

In relation to fixing techniques, paragraph 4.1.1. read

"It is . . . essential that joints of an absolute minimum of ¹⁄₁₆ in be left between the tiles to receive the grouting . . . material. Wider joints may be necessary where the tiles have to conform to a building module or where the composition of the tiles makes such tolerance necessary".

Paragraph 4.2.4. stated

"Tiles should be evenly buttered and tapped back firmly into position in order to ensure that the bed is solid against the whole of the back of the tile including the corners. The resultant thickness of the bed behind the tiles should generally be ¼ in but in no circumstances should it be more than ½ in thick. Uniform spaces between tiles, which should not be less than ¹⁄₁₆ in may be obtained by using insertable spacer pegs which should be inserted as the work proceeds".

Paragraph 4.6.1. listed the general properties of an ideal grout as including "a low shrinkage" and "low compressive strength"; two properties which together would produce flexibility. Paragraph 4.6.2. advised that grout should be "applied with a squeegee working back and forth over the area until all the joints are completely filled". 4.7. read "Tolerance – the surface of the finished tiling shall not vary from the general plane by more than plus or minus ¹⁄₁₆ in in any distance of 6 ft (one in 1 200)".

In the month following publication of CP 212 and, therefore, shortly before the Research Association's letter of 7 August, the British Ceramic Tile Council published *Recommended Methods of Fixing Frost-Resistant Ceramic Wall Tiles*. Under "Materials" it described CTF2 as "a thin-bed adhesive which must not be used in a thickness exceeding ⅛ in", Bal-mix is a mortar which might be "used in thicknesses up to ½ in. and . . . "therefore acceptable where a thick-bed cannot be avoided, such as . . . when the background is uneven" and Bal-flex as "a water based two-compound material . . . developed primarily to give . . . adhesion in . . . difficult conditions . . . e.g. background movement, temperature fluctuations, etc.". Bal-grout was recommended for grouting because of its compressibility and excellent water resistance, but as an alternative an approved water-resistant grouting material might be specified.

Under movement joints the Tile Council's publication recommended at paragraph 3.1. that their position should be decided at the design stage and that they usually be located "in large tiled areas at 10 ft to 15 ft centres, horizontally and vertically". Paragraph 3.2. gave as some general considerations that "joints should extend completely through the tile adhesive bed at least and be continuous in character and should be at least ¼ in wide".

Under 'Detailed Specifications for the Fixing of Frost-Resistant Tiles" the Recommendations stated at paragraph 4.1.

"All exterior installations must be designed to prevent moisture from collecting behind the tile work. Careful attention must be paid at the design stage to the provision of adequate flashing, coping and damp-proof courses . . . The whole of the back of the tile should be in good contact with the adhesive and there should be no air pockets behind . . . joints of at least ¹⁄₁₆ in should be left

round every tile. In a properly designed and correctly tiled installation, moisture is unlikely to penetrate very deeply. Even if water
did succeed in entering, say because of defective grouting, this
would still be much less likely to promote failure if all the tiles are
solidly bedded and there were no voids left behind in which the
water could persist."

Paragraph 4.4. referred to fixing with Bal-mix. It stated that its
backing might be concrete "preferably rendered", that it should only
be specified where the rendering was so uncertain that it would not be
possible to employ CTF2, and that Bal-mix could be used at bed
thickness of up to ½ in maximum, the rendering being soundly
adherent to the backing.

There is no direct evidence that the architects read either CP212 or
the Tile Council's *Recommendations* in 1967, but, since both were mentioned in contractual documents produced by them in 1968, I infer that
they did so.

On 21 September the architects wrote to BAL expressing concern
about joints between tiles and asking about the water-proofing
properties of Bal-grout, Bal-grout with a water-proofing adhesive and
Bal-epoxy, each of which they stated that they would want in black.
BAL replied stating that Bal-grout was suitable for the architects' purpose, had sufficient resistance to withstand the action of water but
would be greatly improved by the addition of a water-proofing additive
such as Sika no 1 and could take a colouring additive. Bal-epoxy was
only available in white.

The architects telephoned the Research Association and received
advice, which the Association confirmed in a letter of 27 September, to
the effect that Bal-mix was a satisfactory adhesive but not flexible and,
therefore, panels should have vertical movement joints in their centres
through the thickness of tiles and adhesive.

Early in November the architects came upon a GLC *Publication &
Materials Bulletin* which referred to tile failures usually caused by differ-
ential movement between tiles and sub-strate (backing) and sometimes
arising where correctly designed and executed joints were included.
The architects sent copies to BAL and to the Research Association.
BAL replied saying that they knew of numerous installations where
rigid adhesives had been used satisfactorily, but that they always
recommended movement joints as laid down in CP 212. The Research
Association wrote saying that the main problem to be met was structural contraction, that adequate joints between tiles, provision of
movement joints and in some cases use of flexible adhesives were
important and that if Bal-mix were used extra provision of movement
joints was advisable.

There is no evidence that the architects ever considered that the tiles would have a substantially shorter life than that of the remainder of the Centre. A letter which they wrote on 13 November 1969 indicated that they expected each to have the same life.

On 19 June 1968 the architects wrote to Wooliscroft informing them that they were inviting tenders for the supply and fixing of their tiles and they caused quantity surveyors on 26 June to invite the sub-contractors to tender.

Terms of a contract had been negotiated with the contractors and, on 9 July, the architects wrote to them informing them of the invitation to the sub-contractors. At no time did the architects confer with or invite observation from the contractors concerning the external use of tiles, of which neither the contractors nor any of their staff had had any experience.

On 27 August the contract for the erection of phase I was made between the University and the contractors. I will later refer to some of its terms. The initial contract drawings issued by the architects did not deal with tiling. The bills of quantities referred to in the contract had been prepared by the architects.

Under bill no 1A tenders for specialist services for which PC sums were included were to be invited by the architects and the contractors were to enter into sub-contracts with the tenderers selected. The item went on to require that the contractors should supervise and organise sub-contractors.

Bill no 2 item A dealt with tolerances in setting out and provided that the contractors should be responsible for the cost of any measures required to rectify departure from the tolerances which were stated as follows:

"On dimensions of 10 ft or over a tolerance of plus or minus ¼ in, and on dimensions of less than 10 ft a tolerance of plus or minus ⅛ in will be allowed.

A tolerance of plus or minus ⅛ in should be permitted on the cross-sectional dimensions of structural members.

The top surface of floor and roof slabs and beams are to be within a ¼ in of the levels and lines shown on the drawings.

Columns and walls are not to be more than ¼ in out of plumb in their storey heights, nor more than ¾ in out of plumb in their full heights".

Finer tolerances had been recommended in November the previous year by Hennessey, Chadwick and Ohcocha & Partners (Hennesseys), structural engineers, who were assisting the architects, but were not adopted, because they would have resulted in an increase in the contract price, as heavier timbers and more bolts would have had to have been used and greater time taken.

No one at the time appreciated what was the cumulative effect of the tolerance provided, but at the trial the experts, Mr Crocker and Mr Kinnear, agreed that it was 1¼ in overall.

On 16 September 1968 the contractors started work on the site. In November Mr Pochin had a discussion with Mr Wright about concrete finish and in a letter of 19 November the architects wrote to the contractors that whilst all structural reinforced concrete should be constructed within the specified tolerances, particular keenness was required in dealing with areas forming a base for tiles. The architects wrote that information regarding tiling would be in their "elemental drawings (460) series", which were ready for issue. Possibly at this time the architects intended that the tolerances for concrete work and tiling should match.

On 17 December 1968 the architects issued an instruction which amounted to a nomination to the contractors to enter into a sub-contract with the sub-contractors on the basis of, among other things, a price schedule of quantities and the series 460 drawings which the contractors had not previously seen.

The schedule at A required that the sub-contractors' prices should include for "any necessary dubbing-out to irregularities in new surfaces on which backings are to be laid", and B that where "Bal-mix and Bal-flex adhesives are specified the tiling is to be applied direct to concrete surfaces which will be constructed within the normal tolerances – the maximum allowed thickness of these adhesives is ½ in and the [sub-contractor] is to achieve a true face within the thickness", and at F that all work will be executed in accordance with CP 212 and the Tile Council's recommendations.

Associated with the 460 drawings was a page of "Tiling – General Notes", which referred to CP 212, stated tile size as 5.9 × 2.9 × ⅜ in and tile module size as 6 × 3 in and gave as positions of tiling expansion (movement) joints:

"In horizontal runs of tiles with no columns, expansion joints to be at 18 ft centres, to coincide with grid line.

In horizontal runs interrupted by columns an expansion joint must be on both sides of the column.

One vertical tiling expansion joint at each floor level".

Tiling expansion joints were to be ¼ in wide. Fixing adhesives were to be Bal-mix on vertical tiling and sills and Bal-flex on soffits, with maximum thickness of ½ in and a minimum of ⅛ in. Tiles were to be pointed with Bal-grout.

The individual drawings showed the locations of structural and tiling expansion joints and how adhesives were to be applied to individual parts of phase I, including windows. Because of the number of tiles that had to be fitted in between movement joints or other fixed points, for example 72 between 18 ft on structural bays, gaps between tiles were about $\frac{1}{16}$ in, made less in places by bunching at ends. The drawings also showed how parapet walls, windowsills and surrounds, soffits and other parts of the building involving tiles were to be formed. Tolerances were much stricter than for the concrete frame.

On 22 January 1969 the contractors placed an order with the tiling sub-contractors, which was followed by a formal sub-contract in the RIBA 1963 Standard Form.

In February 1969 the sub-contractors erected a sample panel on site and, according to Mr Pochin, encountered problems in using Bal-mix in a thick bed. The architects were aware of the test panel. In about April sample panels were erected at Woolliscrofts' premises, principally to enable the architects to consider the colour of Bal-grout with additives. They obviously became concerned that Bal-grout could not be made sufficiently black.

At a site meeting on 11 June 1969, Mr Pochin said that the sub-contractors were awaiting instructions with regard to grout and reminded the architects that tiling was about to begin. On 10 July the architects wrote to BAL saying that they had decided that "on grounds of appearance and workability" a fondu based material was to be preferred, but sought certain assurances, including that the grout would have "reliable weathering characteristics". BAL replied on 17 July saying that the grouting had been developed specially for the Centre, that they had been unable to examine it over a long period of time and that, whilst they were reasonably confident that it would perform quite satisfactorily, they could not give an assurance concerning its long-term durability.

On 24 July 1969, which was two days after tiling had begun, the architects wrote again to BAL asking specifically whether the fondu grout would be water-proof as Bal-grout was or whether water would pass through it with consequent risk of frost damage. On 28 July BAL wrote saying that they anticipated that the fondu-based grout would be water-resistant but not waterproof and that, therefore, water would pass through the joints and since Bal-mix and Bal-flex were also water-resistant, adhesive problems should not arise. They once more stressed their lack of long experience of fondu grout.

On 1 August 1969 the architects wrote to BAL saying that they were satisfied regarding the physical properties of fondu-based grout; thereby giving their approval to grout which they had been told was not water-resistant. On 26 September 1969 the architects issued architects' instruction (AI) 110 to the contractors requesting them to instruct the sub-contractors to grout the whole of the external wall tiling with fondu grout no 1 and as a result the sub-contractors did so.

On 8 and 10 October 1969 the sub-contractors wrote to the contractors referring to many problems with tiling. In particular they stated that neither Bal-mix nor Bal-fix was suitable for fixing tiles to soffits in ¾ in thicknesses as it would not hold the tiles. The matter was referred to the architects, who on 13 November 1969 changed their specification by instructing that CTF2 should be used on the large soffits.

From the commencement, Mr Roper, the clerk of works, was on site every working day, except on Saturdays and during his holidays. Mr Duncan, Hennesseys' resident engineer, was also on site. Neither, however, seems to have concerned himself much with standards of concreting, although Mr Roper thought that they were poor. On 24 June 1969 the architects, who made regular visits, wrote to Hennesseys, saying that the standard of finish so far had been disappointing and that in future Mr Roper would be personally responsible to them for the maintenance of standards and would be involved in fabrication of shutters and inspection before concrete was poured. Hennesseys were asked to co-operate and they did so until Mr Duncan was withdrawn.

From then onwards on phase I and later on phase II Mr Roper, whoever was the engineer at the time and the architects were alert to ensure that the structure was within tolerances at all times. Mr Roper said that each concrete area to be tiled was thoroughly checked for plumbness, alignment and level and that from time to time areas were condemned that had to be done again. Both Mr Pochin and Mr Booth confirmed that supervision was keen. In addition, they said that the contractors' own engineer checked what was done and that there were occasions when the contractors demolished concrete and poured it afresh without being prompted.

Mr Pochin said that parapet walls were formed by raising formwork above levels required to form the main structure of the building. He explained that concreting is not an exact science and that it was extremely difficult to pour concrete to precisely the required heights. He said that concrete was also liable to slump. He thought that the height achieved could reasonably be 1 in out and require building up.

Mr Roper did not remember noticing that walls were formed to incorrect heights, but all were built up by the sub-contractors prior to tiling.

Mr Pochin said that the north boundary gutter to Cornbrook House, which the University pointed out had been made 4⅝ in too low and built up with brickwork, must have been the subject of a specific agreement to that effect since it was so obvious that no one could have failed to see it.

Mr Roper was generally satisfied with the concrete surfaces achieved by the contractors. He said in his proofs given to the University and to the architects that the sub-contractors "did draw my attention from time to time to the undulating surface – I did not think that this condition was sufficiently serious to give rise to a complaint against the contractors – I had seen worse concreting". Mr Pochin said that the contract did not differ from others.

Mr Roper stated that before any tiling actually commenced he checked the area to be tiled with the sub-contractors' foreman, Mr Morgan, and any deviation was brought to the attention of the architect. Surfaces sometimes had to be improved by scabbling or dubbing. Care was taken to ensure that every effort had been made to remove mould oil, which had been used by the contractors as a release agent.

At a meeting on 8 August 1969 the sub-contractors complained that it was impossible for them to produce a finished tile face true in line and plumbness, since the design allowed them a tolerance of ⅛ in where the contractors were allowed ¼ in. The architects told them that by using the thick bed properties of Bal-mix they could achieve the required accuracy without exceeding maximum bed thicknesses.

On 4 September 1969 the sub-contractors complained to the contractors of the discrepancies and variance of concrete on which they had to work. This time the answer was dubbing, which had been provided for in the sub-contract. From then onwards the sub-contractors carried out dubbing more or less continuously in order to achieve backings to which they could fix tiles within the tolerances demanded of them. Applications were thin on soffits, but often much thicker elsewhere. No one suggested using lathing or netting to strengthen the dubbing.

Dubbings should always have been with sand and cement, with a bonding agent, Sealobond, added when appropriate. Sometimes, however, the sub-contractors used Bal-mix instead.

The use of Bal-mix for dubbing as well as an adhesive resulted on occasions in its being more than ½ in thick, contrary to the manufacturer's recommendations and to the tiling specification. No doubt it was easier for the sub-contractors to use Bal-mix only, rather than first use sand and cement and then Bal-mix. Mr Pochin considered this use of Bal-mix to be practical and said that the architects were aware of it.

On a few occasions tilers saved themselves work when dubbing by inserting pieces of of blockwood and the like. This was completely wrong and no one has sought to justify it. On the sub-contractors having what they considered to be a satisfactory surface, they proceeded to tile.

According to Mr Roper whether the sub-contractors were dealing with vertical or horizontal faces, soffits or parapets, they followed broadly the same procedure, namely, first selecting an area to be tiled, placing a timber lath or plank at its base, resting on the timber the appropriate number of tiles to be fixed spaced by judgment and fixing the lower horizontal line of tiles, then vertical tiles at each end and at intermediate positions and afterwards filling in the spaces which had been left. Mr Roper thought, I think mistakenly, that on phase I tiles were applied to adhesive beds, that on phase II they were buttered. After all tiles in the area had been fixed, the spaces between them were grouted. If an area were incomplete at the end of a day the sub-contractors placed sand along the top course, which they should have removed before recommencing work next day.

Mr Roper explained that so far as the many demands on his time permitted he did his best to supervise the sub-contractors. Tiles were always properly fixed when he was present; sometimes he tapped them afterwards with a key to check whether they were adhering properly. On a very few occasions he pulled tiles off to discover whether or not they were properly bedded. He thought that some tilers were less skilled than others and he made complaints to Mr Morgan. He noted that labourers had been employed to do much of the grouting. In a vivid answer Mr Roper described the difficulty involved in supervision: ". . . you cannot stand on the same platform as (the workmen) are on, as they would be embarrassed. If you stand away you do not see what is happening".

The architects should also have inspected the sub-contractors' work as it proceeded, but not as frequently as would Mr Roper, since they were not permanently on the site and they were entitled to rely on Mr Roper doing his work properly.

The contractors appreciated that they were under an obligation to supervise the work of the tiling sub-contractors and all other sub-contractors. Normally the supervision was provided by their general foreman.

It was apparent, however, that Mr Pochin regarded tiling as being something very special, of which the contractors lacked knowledge, and in respect of which they had, therefore, to rely heavily upon the expertise of the sub-contractors. Mr Pochin said that he would have expected a supervisor to have noticed if fewer tiles were fixed than should have been or if there were gaps between the tiles after grouting had been carried out, but not whether there were gaps behind the tiles.

Mr Booth felt no hesitation about supervising the sub-contractors; he thought that everybody on the site should supervise everybody else's work – the more eyes the better. The contractors obtained and studied BAL's literature, but they neither obtained nor looked at CP 212, which was mentioned in the contract documents and would have increased their understanding of tiling and appreciation of what to look for when supervising. Mr Booth was, however, well aware that adhesive needed to be applied all over the backs of tiles.

On 24 September 1969 the architects wrote to the contractors at the instance of Mr Roper complaining about many matters, including careless stripping of formwork and of operatives not being sufficiently aware of the need for high standards of finish. On 13 November 1969 the architects in a letter of that date, to which I have already referred, drew the contractors' attention to the fundamental importance of achieving workmanship of the highest quality to make quite certain that the tiles "will remain in place throughout the lifetime of the building".

On 1 January 1970 the contractors wrote to the architects and, after referring to the amount of dubbing out which had been necessary, submitted that because of tolerances for the structure and the prescribed maximum thickness of adhesive, the University should be responsible for paying for dubbing. The architects passed the letter to the quantity surveyors without comment and the quantity surveyors allowed the sub-contractors payment for dubbing on day work sheets, but at rates lower than those claimed. Mr Pochin believed that about £5 500 was claimed and about £4 000 was paid; he did not think that the contractors paid anything to the sub-contractors.

On 15 January 1970 the architects complained to the contractors that they were not preventing water from pouring through holes in expansion joints into the structure at all levels. No complaints were made about the sub-contractors' work; on 20 April the architects reported to the University's construction sub-committee that they were "doing a first class job".

By June 1970 white staining began to appear on the grouting and tile face. The architects sought BAL's help, who reported that the staining material was almost wholly calcium carbonate. On 23 June the architects wrote to the contractors asserting that the calcium carbonate must have come from concrete surfaces which they had failed to protect.

On 24 June 1970 Mr Pochin replied on behalf of the contractors expressing the view that the staining was caused by concrete drying out through the porous joints of the tiling; he commented that if the joints were so porous, water would soak in as well as out and that staining could occur in the future. By letter of the 29 June 1970 the architects disagreed; they must have forgotten the Research Association's letter of 7 August 1967, which had warned that if a cement based grout were used, white stains would occur.

Staining became widespread; at a meeting to discuss this problem in September 1970 a representative of the Building Research Station was reported to have associated it with "construction water" trapped within the concrete. Mr Booth told me that he repeatedly said to the architects and to others that water behind the tiles could lead not merely to staining, but to tile failure. The problem of staining continued and no satisfactory method of removing the stains has ever been devised. To some extent the staining has weathered.

In 1970 the University decided that it would proceed with phase II of the Centre, using the same architects and contractors. The sub-contractors were asked to tender and in comments upon their tender the quantity surveryors wrote, with a copy to the architects, "we are aware of the difficulties you have experienced on stage I with regard to dubbing out required because of the concrete tolerances but we were not aware of any particular difficulties in the actual fixing of the tiles. . . . You will be reimbursed for the dubbing out authorised by the architect through the contract and by [the contractors] where dubbing out is necessary because of their concrete work exceeding the permitted tolerances". On 31 December the quantity surveyors wrote to the tiling sub-contractors: "If any dubbing out is required by the architect during the course of the contract this will be dealt with as a variation".

Mr Pochin and Mr Booth urged the architects in view of the staining which had occurred to change the grout to be used on phase II, but they refused. Mr Pochin, said that the architects in the person of Mr Wright, resented any criticisms or suggestions about the design. On 17 November 1970 the sub-contractors wrote to the quantity surveyors saying that they had suggested during phase I through the clerk of works that epoxy resin grout rather than Fondu grout no 1 should be used, since in their opinion the Fondu was not waterproof and might be washed out, but the architects had rejected the suggestion.

On 8 April 1971 the contract for phase II was made between the University and the contractors. It was substantially the same as that for phase I. In the bills of quantities under "nominated sub-contractors" there was an item regarding supervision and administration of sub-contracts. Dimensional tolerances were stated by reference to reference grids; the effect of them as agreed by Mr Crocker and Mr Kinnear was to make the maximum cumulative tolerance 9/16 in. Lime was removed from the concrete specification, as the architects believed that it was a source of staining.

The architects nominated the sub-contractors, the contractors gave their order on 23 April and the sub-contractors entered into a sub-contract. The schedule of quantities for phase II repeated the requirements of the earlier contract, except that from the first Fondu no 2 was specified. It was stated that the concrete surfaces to which tiling would be attached would be within "normal tolerances". A note stated that no allowance had been made for dubbing out. Drawings followed.

From February 1971 work had been proceeding on both phases I and II. On phase II Ove Arup were the engineers and visited almost daily. On 19 February 1971 the sub-contractors wrote to the contractors point out that a dwarf wall was not necessarily waterproof because the tile was not fully vitrious and the fondu grout was absorbent. The contractors passed the letter to the architects inviting comments, but received none. Mr Booth said that he had made similar criticisms of other walls earlier.

In March certain sill tiles fell from the north elevation of Cornford House and had to be put right. The tiling sub-contractors had failed to insert expansion joints as shown on the drawings. The tile fall came to the knowledge of Mr Thomas, who wrote on 5 May 1971 a sharp letter to the architects, saying that he understood that "in spite of all the detailed cross-examination at the design stage, and assurances that were given to the University, external tiles had fallen off the walls of the building". The architects replied taking exception to the tone of Mr Thomas's letter, saying that the tile failure related to only a very small proportion of the tiling and promising a report. On 19 May 1971 the report was provided: it indicated that there had been trouble on the south wall as on the north and blamed the tiling sub-contractors and said that no further problems were expected.

Phase I was completed except for snagging in about July 1971 and students moved into Crawford House in September 1971. Other accommodation was gradually occupied. Soon after tiles were fixed on phase II, stains appeared. In October 1971 the architects became aware of a risk of water penetration and frost damage due to the method of tiling window sills shown on their drawings. Difficulties occurred with the tiling of soffits. Dubbing took place pursuant to instructions and in a letter of 6 December to Mr Thomas the architects explained that experience of phase I showed that it would be required. It had been thought that separate instructions for it would give greater control of it.

On 6 April 1972 the sub-contractors wrote to the contractors making fresh criticisms of the design of the tops of the parapet wall and referring to water penetration, which on the following day the contractors passed to the architects. On this occasion the architects replied stating that they did not accept that the position was as stated by the sub-contractors.

On 26 April 1972 the sub-contractors complained to the quantity surveyors of their difficulties in tiling over asphalt at the bottom of the flat roof sides of parapet walls. On 27 April the architects issued an instruction that tiles fixed to asphalt with Bal-flex be removed and the asphalt be treated with Sealo-bond and cement before the tiles were refixed with Bal-mix. Letters of BAL dated 27 April and 30 May indicated that to the best of their knowledge Bal-flex should adhere to asphalt and that they had no experience of fixing tiles to a slurry.

On 22 May 1972 the quantity surveyors wrote to the architects stating that to date the cost of dubbing was approximately £4000, whereas only £1557 had been anticipated altogether. On 29 June the University enquired why it was necessary for them to pay for such a large amount of dubbing and asking whether it was due to bad cambers, etc due to bad casting of concrete, etc. On 13 July the quantity surveyors replied agreeing that there was a large amount of dubbing, all of which was authorised by the architects. They said that it was required to overcome permitted tolerances in the concrete structure and particular problems at windows and shop fronts; any dubbing out because of contractors' workmanship was not included.

In about October 1972 the architects authorised the contractors to release retention monies in respect of phase I to the sub-contractors and they did so. The contractors have either destroyed or lost many of their documents from this period and there is no evidence that they first obtained an indemnity from the sub-contractors in respect of latent defects. Between 26 February and 16 October 1973 phase II was completed and the University took possession of it in five stages and the building was gradually occupied.

In the Autumn of 1972 some tiles had become loose on Cornbrook House, fifth level, near to the bridge, but the defect was attributed by the architects to the sub-contractors having tiled across an expansion joint. In May 1973 tiles on Cornbrook House, third level, were found by the clerk of works to be "addled", that is to say hollow sounding when tapped, so indicating loss of adhesion. The tiling sub-contractors eventually replaced them.

On 10 July 1973 the architects wrote to Mr Crosby, who had by then taken over from Mr Thomas, informing him that the tiling sub-contractors' account for dubbing amounted to £15000, which was much more than had been anticipated and which they were still investigating. On 30 July 1973 Mr Crosby wrote expressing the view that it would be unreasonable for the University to be charged the full cost.

Arguments then ensued between quantity surveyors, sub-contractors, architects and contractors: not as to the amount of dubbing, about which there could be do dispute since daywork sheets had been signed by the clerk of works, but about rates and who should pay. Eventually the tiling sub-contractors agreed to reduce their rates. On 19 March the following year the architects wrote to the contractors alleging that certain flank walls had been "built so far out of tolerance that a great deal of dubbing out was necessary to make anything like a satisfactory job possible."

Finally, the University paid about £11000 to the tiling sub-contractors. The contractors paid approximately £1700 to them on the basis that reflected the amount by which their work was out of tolerance; it represented 13.3 per cent of the total amount of dubbing. Mr Pochin said that the majority of the dubbing for which the contractors paid was in relation to toilet ducts. They paid believing that the tolerances applicable were stricter than they in fact were.

The sub-contractors who fixed balustrading and lightning conductor cables to the tops of parapet walls on both phases I and II did so by drilling holes through the tiles, inserting plugs and screwing into the plugs so as to attach clips. This was in accordance with drawings issued under the authority of the architects. Mr Booth said that he expressed to the architects and the clerk of works his concern with regard to this method of fixing the cables because he believed that it would lead to water ingress, but that they did not pay any attention to him.

On about 16 August 1973 a University employee noticed loose tiles above an entrance to Crawford House and, instead of reporting them to his employers, or to the architects, reported them to the city engineer, who served a dangerous structure notice upon the University! In a flurry of activity the contractors took down the tiles. In September 1973 another area of tiles on phase II showed signs of failure. On 10 October 1973 the architects urged the tiling sub-contractors to put both defective areas right by the 17 October when the University Council was due to inspect.

In November 1973 the sub-contractors sought to discover why tiles had failed and were advised by Sealocrete Group Sales Ltd, whose laboratories had examined specimens, that the failures were due to prolonged saturation. BAL gave similar advice. The tiling sub-contractors passed the reports which they had obtained to the architects. The University were not informed.

In January 1974 the architects considered that tiling at the foot of parapet walls on phase II was suspect. In February 1974 the architects were advised by Lionel Arnold (Tile Fixing) Ltd, whom they had consulted that tile failures were due to salt expansion behind tiles caused by water building up in small reservoirs in the tile joints. A remedial list prepared by the architects in February 1974 required work to tiling in several locations on phase II, so did several subsequent letters and a note of a joint inspection by the architects and contractors in April 1974 recorded defective tiling. On 19 June 1974 the tiling sub-contractors claimed that they had replaced rendering and tiles were requested.

In 1975 the tiling appeared to be generally satisfactory; photographs taken by Mr Thompson do not show anything as being wrong. Mr Crosby thought that the problems of 1973 had been overcome and when in October Mr Daggett became responsible for the Centre and began to visit it weekly, he did not see anything to cause him concern. The University assumed responsibility for day-to-day maintenance of the Centre.

On 21 July 1975 the sub-contractors requested release of retention monies and on 9 February 1976 the architects wrote to the contractors stating that a certificate of indemnity would first be required from the sub-contractors. On 20 February the contractors wrote to the sub-contractors requesting an indemnity and suggesting how it should be worded. The sub-contractors replied on 25 February 1976 and under the heading "University of Manchester Precinct Centre Phase II" used the suggested words:

> "We hereby indemnify you against any costs in which you may be involved, whether directly or indirectly in respect of, or the rectification of, any defects (including latent defects or any omissions) as regards the work, materials or goods executed or supplied by us and which may be discovered after the certification of final payment to us, provided that we shall first be given the opportunity of ourselves rectifying any defects (including any latent defects or any omissions) in our own work, materials or goods".

On 16 March 1976 the contractors passed the sub-contractors' letter to the architects describing it as "an indemnity to our satisfaction". On or about 25 March the architects agreed to the release of the phase II tiling retention monies and the contractors paid them to the sub-contractors.

From time to time the University made payments to the contractors, which included monies related to tiling, but no final certificate has ever been issued to the contractors in respect of phases I or II.

Unhappily two days before the sub-contractors provided the indemnity letter which led to the release of the retention monies some tiles fell from a part of phase II on to the pavement of Oxford Road. Mr Daggett immediately arranged to safeguard pedestrians and for other tiles in the neighbourhood which appeared loose, 64 in all, to be taken down. Whether the architects had learnt of the fall before they gave consent to the release of the retention monies I do not know.

Between March and October 1976 there were no major tile failures, but there were signs that some might occur. The University requested the architects to inspect the area of failed tiling and on 8 October they wrote saying that the failure was probably caused by the ingress of water behind the tiling. It was becoming increasingly apparent to Mr Daggett and to others that voids and channels were frequent behind tiles, which had not been fully bedded. Mr Daggett thought also that there should have been more expansion joints. On 15 October Mr Crosby wrote to the architects saying that the University was more concerned about the condition of the tiling than they were; as he explained, he was endeavouring to hand back the problem of the tiling to the architects and contractors.

The architects sent two samples of tile to Harry Stanger Ltd's laboratory, who commented among other things upon the Bal-mix attached to them being ¾ in thick, and recommended an overall survey by tapping for hollowness. The architects sent the report to Mr Crosby and after meetings between their Mr Neil and Mr Daggett and correspondence Stangers were instructed to carry out tests at prescribed locations on phase II. On 30 June 1978 they reported that tapping had proved a sure test of bonding, that they had found many loose tiles, that grout was generally in good condition and that in some areas large quantities of water were stored behind the tiles and would lead to failure. Mr Crosby recognised that the University was faced with a major problem. The architects informed the contractors and tiling sub-contractors.

There were further falls of tiles on phase II, including some on the north side, and in the interest of safety the University had to remove other tiles. The architects sought advice from Ove Arup and from BAL each of whom inspected the building. On 19 October 1978 Ove Arup, after excluding movement of the building as a cause of failure, reported finding a preponderance of tile to backing failure, evidence of leaching which could only have been due to water behind the tile face and finding horizontal layers of pure sand at each horizontal tile bed. Also on 19 October BAL reported that calcium carbonate from the concrete structure might have interfered with the development of adhesion, that some concrete had been contaminated with oil or with a release agent, that there had been small voids present at the interface between adhesive and concrete, permitting penetration of water, and that in some places Bal-mix had, because of the surface of the concrete, been applied in two coats, a practice which they did not endorse. The two reports were passed to Mr Crosby.

The architects sought a further opinion from Lionel Arnold, which was provided on 11 January 1979. Lionel Arnold thought that the major contributory factor in the tile failure was the almost butt jointing of the tiling, commented that window details could have been designed so as to shed water better, and recommended *inter alia*, aluminium trims over parapets and the cutting of expansion joints at centres not greater than 8 ft. The Lionel Arnold report was not sent to Mr Crosby.

After receiving Ove Arup's and BAL's reports the University decided to seek advice from a source other than the architects. They instructed Mr Crocker, then of Bickerdike Allen & Partners, who inspected phase II on 21 November 1979. In December Mr Crosby and Mr Daggett, who had himself prepared a comprehensive and thoughtful report, visited Warwick and Birmingham Universities, at each of which tile failures had occurred and buildings had been reclad mainly with aluminium sheets supported on steel or phosphor bronze backs. They did not like what they saw and in particular they noticed that cladding at ground level had been damaged. They thought that turbulence due to tall buildings at Manchester might cause sheets to become detached. In December also the University sent an apologetic letter to tenants and occupiers of phase II and then erected scaffolding around it.

In January 1979 Mr Crocker submitted his first report, based partly on his inspection and partly on information derived from other reports. He considered that major physical causes of the tile failures were lack of adhesion of bedding to substrate, water behind tiles, lack of adhesion between grout and tiles, presence of sand, uneven substrate and contamination on concrete faces. The latter was not based on his own observation.

Mr Crocker thought that architects, contractors and sub-contractors were each in some respects responsible for the failure. He recommended a detailed survey of phase I. He thought that the possibilities for remedial action were: to remove all tiling and retile to an improved specification; to remove all tiles and apply a wet finish (that is to say a rendering) to substrates; and to apply an independent sheet cladding. He considered that the third was the only viable answer. He advised that all solutions would involve alterations to window detailing.

On 21 May 1980 Mr Crocker inspected phase I in company with members of the University. They found tile failures and concluded that phase I would start to behave in a similar way to phase II. In March 1980 the University sent sections of Mr Crocker's report to the architects, who in June 1980 declined to issue a final certificate relating to phase II because of investigations into tile failures. No final certificates have ever been issued. At meetings in June and July between representatives of the architects and of the University the former objected strongly to criticisms of them in the Crocker report and to what they described as "the drastic and costly remedies recommended in it". Further and more substantial failures of tiles occurred and in August part of Booth Street had to be closed temporarily.

In September 1980 Mr Crocker wrote to Mr Crosby urging speedy remedial action and in September and October the University obtained estimates of an illustrative character from two companies who were suppliers of metal cladding. The University obtained a second opinion from Sir Donald Gibson CBE, FRIBA, FRTPI, who in an admirably short and to the point report, expressed the view that the design was over-optimistic and criticised it, made some criticisms of workmanship, thought that the situation would get worse, and recommended removal of all the tiles and treatment of the concrete structure with a textured external paint. Sir Donald's last recommendation was unfortunately based on a false premise, as he believed that the concrete was weatherproof, so that even without tiles it would keep dry internally. Sir Donald ended his report with the words: "I have not recommended a tile replacement solution, and I would not do so." Mr Crosby sought further assistance from Sir Donald, who suggested that possible solutions be tried out on small areas.

Both Mr Crocker and Sir Donald had advised against retiling and Mr Daggett and Mr Crosby were firmly of the same view. At a meeting on 28 November 1979 Mr Crosby told Mr Armstrong that in the light of the second opinion which the University had obtained remedial action could no longer be delayed, and that there was no prospect of the University agreeing to a tile replacement programme which was advocated by the architects. On 5 December 1979 the architects wrote urging the University not to rush.

On 7 January 1980 the first serious falls of tiles from phase I occurred when a tile narrowly missed hitting a pedestrian; soon afterwards some tiles were taken down and protective scaffolding erected.

Mr Crosby aided by Mr Daggett considered whether a paint solution to the Centre's problems could be adopted. They seem not to have had in mind that the concrete was not weatherproof, but they decided against the use of paint because of the difficulties which would be involved in first removing dubbing and adhesive, the noise and dirt which would be created for tenants and occupiers, including the students, during such removal, the risk of shadows arising from undulating surfaces, difficulties in matching the appearance created by paint with that of nearby buildings and the need for substantial future maintenance, requiring cradles and scaffolds. Later they came to realise that the use of mechanical tools to remove dubbing and the like would have created considerable vibration.

On 16 January 1980 the University instructed Mr Gibbon to produce proposals for cladding the external tiled areas of the Centre. He studied Mr Crocker's and Sir Donald's reports, had discussions with officers of the University and with Ove Arup and visited Birmingham and Warwick. On 14 April 1980 Mr Gibbon advised that retiling would not be a reliable method of refacing. He recommended the recladding of walls with brickwork supported on fixings secured to the structure and the use of metal sheeting on window sills, other modelled surfaces and the bridge. The solid wall would encase tiled areas and prevent loose tiles from causing injury, would cope with what he called "unavoidable" lack of precision in the structure, it would have a life of at least 50 years and, if made of red brick, would harmonise with the remainder of the Centre and with nearby buildings. He suggested that repairs be carried out in sections, so that areas most urgently in need of repair could be dealt with first, making tenants' problems more manageable and permitting work to be done by small closely co-ordinated teams.

Mr Gibbon submitted with his own report one by Mr Seward of Michael Seward and Partners, quantity surveyors, which supported his recommendations. Mr Seward thought that in choosing refacing materials the prime consideration was to keep the tenants in occupation, as, if they had to be relocated temporarily, cost would be severely compounded. He advised that cost advantage would be gained if the tiled surfaces could be retained in position behind any new facing material. He thought that brickwork had never relinquished its cost advantage as a combined structure and facing material. Mr Seward recommended that a retiling solution be costed for comparison or "betterment" purposes.

On 24 April 1980 the University authorised Mr Gibbon to proceed to prepare a detailed scheme. Mr Gibbon prepared initial drawings, upon which Mr Crosby commented. Sir Donald gave general approval of the Gibbon concepts, but once again suggested trying out possible solutions. Mr Crocker also approved. On 25 June 1980 the city engineer expressed the opinion that a brick solution seemed to be the most advantageous and that he did not consider that it would materially alter the appearance of the Centre so as to require planning permission. The University gave authority for a trial scheme to be carried out.

A contract was entered into with J. Jarvis & Sons Ltd to secure areas of tiles with bituthene sheeting, erect brick cladding at such a distance from the tiles, dubbing or structure as to form a cavity, support the brick walls on steel angles and attach them to the structure by steel ties and provide anodised aluminium window surrounds all to a height of approximately four storeys at the eastern end of Crawford House. Work began in October 1980 and took until March 1981.

Setting out positions were established from plumb-lines dropped from roof parapet level and measurements taken to the tile or brick faces. Deviations were generally between $\frac{1}{8}$ and $\frac{5}{16}$ apart from one line on the Booth Street frontage where the building was found to lean outwards by $1\frac{7}{16}$ in between the ground and third levels. There were also deviations ranging from $\frac{1}{2}$ in to $1\frac{1}{2}$ in in the vertical line-up of windows and the squareness of their reveals. It was not possible to be certain whether the face of the building reflected the original structure or as dubbed or hacked. Mr Gibbon had the impression that the concrete surfaces beneath tiles and dubbing were not plumb or vertical, but that was only an impression. Because of the deviations the steel angles used had to be of varying sizes, there had to be some packing and aluminium elements had to be cut and trimmed individually.

To reduce disturbance to occupants drilling of the structure was restricted to specified hours. The new brickwork harmonised with the old. There was a change in modelling in that the new brickwork protruded beyond the old, whereas the tiles had been inset, but the result was aesthetically satisfactory. The test contract cost more than had been anticipated, partly because of the the structural irregularities. The addition of the brick cladding provided a second waterproof barrier to the building and improved its thermal quality, but in the opinion of Mr Gibbon only marginally.

In 1981 some tiles which had been fixed to what Mr Crosby

described as very good and accurate concrete proved on tapping to be hollow and had to be replaced.

In March 1982 Jarvis carried out a laser survey of levels 4 to 8 of the north elevation of Crawford House. In October they carried out a similar survey of levels 1 to 3 of the same elevation. In September 1983 they carried out a survey of the west elevation of Crawford House. Mr Collings, who as general foreman participated in the former and as site manager arranged the two latter, produced drawings showing the results and illustrative sections based on them. They showed that the face of the building was not completely vertical: in places it was recessed and in others protruded. In a considerable number of locations the difference exceeded ¼ in.

Mr Collings agreed with Mr Patrick Garland that the surveys were taken roughly ten years after the building was completed and that any building, however well founded or built, would have tended to have moved during that time if only because concrete shrinks under load. Mr Collings also agreed that all measurements were taken from an arbitrary plane. Mr Pochin demonstrated that by selecting a different setting-out line for the laser different results would have been achieved.

In June 1980 the University, having concluded that the test contract had been successful, decided to proceed with further works to the Centre, at a pace governed primarily by financial considerations, but also by the desirability of keeping tenants and others in occupation of the Centre, so that noise, vibration and activity were kept to a minimum. Mr Gibbon prepared detailed remedial drawings. In 1982 works similar to the test works were carried out to the remainder of the Booth Street aspect of Crawford House and metal copings were provided for the parapets: these were followed by works involving the use of heavy gauge metal on the bridge. Other works are proceeding gradually. At the same time more tiles are becoming loose and some fall.

The experts agreed that the Centre would have a life of 75 or more years; the tiling if all technical errors had been avoided initially might have lasted 25 to 30 years; and the polysulphide in the movement joints 10 years. If the tiles had been simply put back without other major changes, they might have lasted between 2 and 7 years. They thought that the phase I tiles had been done well.

Mr Wear gave evidence of costs incurred by the University to date in connection with the tiling, namely:

For road divisions and the like	£ 1 267.45
Hire of scaffolding	£ 83 521.67
Payments for occasional repairs (exc. paintwork)	£ 11 930.32
Payment to Jarvis for remedial work	£455 870.00
Professional fees	£ 76 477.66
Estimated proportion of clerk of work's salary	£ 7 000.00
Estimated proportion of Mr Daggett's salary	£ 8 000.00
Professional advisers' plans, etc. including VAT	£ 9 660.0
Total	£653 727.10

No VAT had been paid upon the cost of the building works as the result of a decision of a VAT Appeal Tribunal.

Mr Seward gave evidence as to estimated future costs of carrying out the brick cladding solution, which I understood to be:

Jarvis including allowance for fluctuations	£1 858 500
Professional fees	£ 343 200
Expenses, documents, site supervision	£ 46 700
VAT at 15 per cent	£ 58 000
	£2 306 400

Doubts exist as to whether VAT will be payable despite the recent Finance Bill. Questions were raised as to whether the University could not proceed with work more speedily and, therefore, cheaply, possibly by borrowing money since its credit is good, but more work at the same time would involve more disturbance to occupants.

Mr Seward also provided hypothetical figures based on 1983 prices for retiling. His figures were arrived at by taking figures which had been agreed earlier with quantity surveyors then instructed on behalf of the architects and adding to them substantial additions of his own. In that way he produced a figure of £1 630 440. Mr Roberts did not agree with Mr Seward; his total figure was £526 339.

The fundamental reason for the disagreement between Mr Seward's and Mr Roberts' figures was that they were prepared on different assumptions as to specification.

Mr Seward assumed a new specification, which would result in a tiling solution which would have some prospect of success. It envisaged among other things stainless steel reinforcement for dubbing, aluminium copings for parapets and an enormous increase in dubbing. Since the design would be different, substantial professional fees would be payable. Mr Seward also assumed that VAT would have to be paid.

Mr Roberts assumed that there would be no change in specification whatsoever. Professional fees would therefore be minimal. He also assumed, perhaps somewhat optimistically, that VAT would not be payable.

Mr Roberts put forward comparable figures to both Mr Seward's and his own for 1973, 1976 and 1978 and Mr Seward agreed the last two.

The University permitted their claims against the architects to be dismissed, but nonetheless I think that the first issue which I must consider is *to what extent did the architects act in breach of contract and/or in breach of duty in negligence to the University?*

I think that in substance the architects' duties to the University in contract and in tort were the same, namely to exercise the skill and care to be expected of a competent architect in designing the Centre, in supervising its construction and, when and if necessary, reviewing and amending the design. The latter obligation certainly lasted until practical completion of the works. Whether it lasted longer and indeed, since no final certificates have been issued, whether it continues, are not matters which I need decide.

The architects not having previously used ceramic tiles on the outsides of buildings were plainly right to seek information as they did. From their visit to the Cambridge Library, the letters which they received and the publications which they read, they should, I think, have learnt:

(1) That tiles were being used externally in this country, but that no one had had long-term experience of them and that some failures had occurred, so that in the use of them particular caution was needed;

(2) That water penetration behind tiles could by itself lead to loss of adhesion or could allow frost action to develop;

(3) That thermal expansion could affect adhesion;

(4) That variations in strength and shrinkages could lead to compressive stresses;

(5) That achievement of concrete surfaces flat enough to take tiles would be difficult and that unless they could be made true within a tolerance of plus or minus ⅛ in dubbing with sand and cement would be necessary;

(6) That if dubbing to a thickness of more than ½ in be required, it should be built up in layers;

(7) That however adhesive be applied it should form a solid bed, so that there would be no air pockets behind the tiles capable of holding water;

(8) That Bal-mix could be used as an adhesive, but not to a greater thickness than ½ in and that it was not flexible;

(9) That dark coloured tiles absorbed heat more than light coloured ones, and should therefore be kept to a minimum;

(10) That gaps were required between tiles of not less than 1/16 in according to CP 212 or 1/12 in according to the Research Association, but should be greater where higher thermal action was to be expected;

(11) That water falling on tiling concentrates on gaps, from which it should be excluded;

(12) That most cement and sand grouts were neither waterproof nor water resistant, that Bal-grout was resistant only and that all could be improved by a waterproofing additive;

(13) That movement/expansion joints at least ¼ in wide were required, that CP 212 recommended joints at storey heights and 10 ft apart vertically, and that the Tile Council recommended them at 10–15 ft horizontally and vertically, and that the Research Association stressed the need for them with Bal-mix; and

(14) That parapet walls should have copings and damp-proof courses.

For architects to use untried, or relatively untried materials or techniques cannot in itself be wrong, as otherwise the construction industry can never make any progress. I think however, that architects who are venturing into the untried or little tried would be wise to warn their clients specifically of what they are doing and to obtain their express approval. The architects in this case mentioned their intention to tile to Mr Thomas, who, while he did not stop them, displayed anxiety about it. I think that it was all the more incumbent upon the arcitects to be careful. The practical impossibility of reconciling tolerances achievable with concrete with those essential for satisfactory tiling might by itself have made the architects uncertain whether tiling would be successful. The University wanted a low maintenance building, and as the architects wrote in their letter of 13 November 1969, they intended that the tiles should last the life of the building. Any doubts about the reliability of tiles should have been resolved by not using them. The architects could have achieved waterproofing and the aesthetic effects at which they were aiming by the use of other materials.

CP 212 and other literature were not binding on the architects in the sense that they were obliged to follow their recommendations precisely, but they should certainly have taken them into account and disregarded them only if they had good scientific reasons for so doing.

The architects' design for phases I and II did not heed the recommendations in that they specified large areas of red tiles on vertical surfaces, soffits, parapet walls and window sills and yet, despite the certainty of thermal movement, they provided only tiny gaps between tiles, which could reduce to nothing with a minor error in setting out, and horizontal/movement joints at 18 ft centres. The certainty of compressive stresses was a further reason for having joints at 10 ft intervals as mentioned in CP 212 and for reasonable gaps between tiles.

The architects designed the Centre without features which would protect tiles from rain. Knowing that water would be concentrated on gaps between tiles, they made the gaps so small that they would be very difficult to grout. After specifying Bal-grout initially, they changed to Fondu no 1 without a waterproofing additive. They persisted in using

Fondu on phase II after staining had occurred on phase I and the contractors had urged a change of grout.

The architects designed the parapet walls without metal copings, when they should have realised that rain or water from snow was certain to pentrate the grout between tiles. Knowing that and also knowing the concrete was not waterproof, they failed to specify damp-proof courses.

Apart from failing to heed the tiling literature, the architects made what can, I think, only be described as elementary mistakes. They required the tiles be taken over slurry over asphalt at parapet walls (as shown on figure 7 to Mr Crocker's report); failed to provide movement joints where surfaces in different planes met (figure 8); designed windows so that tile sills were brought against the face of the window and not so that vertical surfaces came down on top of the tiles mastering them, thus creating water paths (figures 10 and 11) and made other similar errors at other locations (figures 12, 13, 14 and 15). In specifying very small gaps between tiles and in their detailing of windows and some other units, they did not have proper regard for buildability.

During phases I and II the architects visited regularly and during their inspections they looked at work which was in progress. Their letter of 24 June 1969 showed that they were concerned about the standard of concreting and no doubt they continued to take a particular interest in it. If, however, it be correct that the concrete was seriously out of tolerance, a question which I will deal with under the third issue, they failed to discover it.

The sub-contractors plainly failed to butter the backs of the tiles correctly, so as not to leave voids, and they allowed sand to remain between some tiling courses. It would seem that on no occasion did the architects discover that the sub-contractors were not doing their work properly. If the areas of tiling had been small and the sub-contractors had worked on site for only a short period, I think that, bearing in mind the problems of supervision highlighted by Mr Roper, the architects might be excused for not having detected the sub-contractors' failures, but since the areas were very extensive and the sub-contractors were working from 1969 to 1972, I must infer that the architects did not inspect properly. In the light of the contractors' evidence I think that the architects must have been aware that Bal-mix was being used in thicknesses exceeding ½ in, contrary to the specification, but they either gave their tacit approval or simply failed to check it. They cannot have concerned themselves with the concrete in the parapet walls.

The architects did not revise their designs in respect of either phase I or phase II. Presumably they believed that problems arising out of the difference between tolerances for concreting and for tiling were being overcome successfully by dubbing and it did not come to their knowledge that the sub-contractors were experiencing difficulty in grouting such narrow gaps between tiles. Large scale failures of tiles on phase II did not occur until the works were almost complete and on phase I not until much later.

On the other hand both Mr Pochin and Mr Booth communicated to the architects their view that the staining which began before the completion of phase I indicated that there should be at least a change in grout, Mr Booth and the sub-contractors criticised the parapet design and Mr Booth complained about the method of fixing lightning conductors. In these last respects the architects cannot I think be excused for having failed to bring about necessary changes in design.

In my opinion the architects acted in breach of contract and negligence in their designs for phases I and II, in their supervision and in their failure to review their design in the respects which I have mentioned.

The architects were the University's agents, but the University had on site the clerk of works, Mr Roper, who was at all important times their employee. I think that it is convenient to take as the second issue *whether Mr Roper exercised care to protect the University's interests?*

Mr Roper was obviously a conscientious and hardworking person, whom the architects thought worthy of their employment, of whom both Mr Perrin and Mr Booth spoke highly and who did not need to be instructed in his general duties by the architects. Unfortunately he had a great deal to do. He was knowledgeable about concreting and about most building work, but he had had no previous experience of external tiling.

Mr Roper told me that after June 1969 he checked all concrete areas and that he always paid considerable attention to tiling. Despite the demands on his time, he had more opportunities for inspection than had the architects.

I think that occasional errors in the concrete structure might have escaped Mr Roper's attention, but that if there were widespread departures from tolerances they could not have done so. Clearly he failed to notice or to attach importance to the concrete in the walls being poured too low.

Making all allowances for problems in supervising workmen and for Mr Roper's other difficulties, I think that he should have discovered that over large areas the tiles were not being buttered properly. He could have pulled off more tiles than the occasional one. He should have insisted upon the removal of sand from tile faces.

I think that to the extent which I have mentioned Mr Roper failed to exercise proper care on behalf of the University.

The third issue is *whether the contractors acted in breach of their contract with the University?* I am not concerned with whether they were negligent, as that is not now alleged against them.

Condition 1(1) of each contract required the contractors to "carry out and complete the works shown upon the Contract drawings and described . . . in the Contract bills . . . to the reasonable satisfaction of the architect". Condition 6(1) provided that "All materials, goods and workmanship shall so far as procurable be of the respective kinds and standards described in the Contract bills".

The University asserted and the contractors admitted subject to a qualification as to tiling that there were implied terms in the contract and that the contractors should carry out the works in a good and workmanlike manner and use good and proper materials.

Condition 1(2) required the contractors to give written notice of any discrepancy between drawings and/or bills, but there was no condition which required the contractors to warn architects as agents of the University of defects in their design.

The University alleged that a duty to warn was to be implied. The contractors did not admit the allegation, but the matter was not argued at length because in *Equitable Debenture Assets Corporation Ltd* v *William Moss and Others* (1984) 2 ConLR 1 I had decided that such a term could be implied.

My conclusion in *Equitable Debenture* was based upon *Duncan* v *Blundell* (1820) 3 Stark 6, Bayley J, and *Brunswick Construction Ltd* v *Nowlan* (1974) 21 BLR 27 (Supreme Court of Canada), both construction cases, and on the application of *The Moorcock* [1889] 14 PD 64 (CA), *Reigate* v *Union Manufacturing Company* [1918] 1 KB 592 (CA) and *Liverpool City Council* v *Irwin* [1977] AC 239 (House of Lords), which deal with implication of terms.

In this case I think that a term was to be implied in each contract requiring the contractors to warn the architects as the University's agents of defects in design, which they believed to exist. Belief that there were defects required more than mere doubt as to the correctness of the design, but less than actual knowledge of errors.

Condition 27(a) of the contracts empowered the architects to nominate, subject to safeguards in favour of the contractors, sub-contractors to be employed by them. Bill no 1A, to which I have referred, was to the same effect. The contractors agreed that if the sub-contractors' workmanship were bad they would be liable in respect of it, since it would give rise to breaches of the contractors' own obligations under the contracts in the same way as would bad workmanship by sub-contractors whom they had selected. Their liability for sub-contractors was however subject to condition 27(e) which read:

"If the Architect desires to secure final payment to any nominated sub-Contractor before final payment is due to the Contractor, and if such sub-Contractor has satisfactorily indemnified the Contractor against any latent defects, then the Architect may in an interim Certificate include an amount to cover the said final payment . . .

Upon such final payment . . . save for latent defects the Contractor shall be discharged from all liability for the work, materials or goods executed or supplied by such sub-Contractor under the sub-Contract".

Condition 27(e) is a standard condition in the JCT contracts, but there is apparently no reported case in which the meaning of "latent" in it has been considered. I was, therefore, referred to shipping cases.

In *The Dimitrios N. Rallias* (1922) 13 Lloyds Rep 363, Lord Sterndale said at p 365 that if a defect "could be discovered by the exercise of ordinary care it cannot be said to be latent" and at p 366 Lord Atkin referred to a definition of latent gathered from American decisions – "a defect which could not be discovered by a person of competent skill and using ordinary care". In *Charles Brown & Co.* v *Nitrate Producers' Steamship Company* (1937) 58 Lloyds Rep 188, Porter J said at p 191: "The only question is whether by "latent" is meant that you have to use every possible method to discover whether it exists, or whether you must use reasonable methods . . . I think it means such an examination as a reasonably careful man skilled in that matter would make . . .".

In *The Caribbean Sea* [1980] 1 Lloyds Rep 338 Robert Goff J at p 348 applied Porter J's words as a test of what was "latent" in the context of a marine insurance policy. I think that they may equally well be used for the purposes of condition 27(e).

Mr Garland submitted that the effect of condition 27(e) was clear: if architects, after contractors have obtained an indemnity from sub-contractors in respect of latent defects, issue an interim certificate which provides for final payment to sub-contractors, the effect is to exempt the contractors from all liability in connection with the sub-contractors' work except in relation to defects in it which are latent.

Mr Knight submitted that condition 27(e) should be construed narrowly, as otherwise it would not be consistent with condition 15(2) and (4), concerning defects which appear during the defects liability period, and condition 30(4) and (7), relating to the exclusion from the conclusiveness of a final certificate of defects not discoverable on reasonable inspection.

I think that condition 27(e) and conditions 15(2) and (4) and 30(4) and (7) are mutually consistent. Before architects issue an interim certificate including final payment to sub-contractors they should make sure that there are no apparent defects in the work done and materials supplied by the sub-contractors. If they then issue the certificate the contractors are released from liability in respect of any defects which might have been discovered on examination by a reasonably careful person skilled in building. The contractors remain liable for latent defects.

If subsequently latent defects manifest themselves, then the contractor can be required to remedy them in accordance with the terms of the contract. If they appear during the defects liability period, they should be dealt with under condition 15. If they appear only after the issue of the final certificate, they may fall within condition 30(7)(b).

Part of bill no 1A expressly provided that "the contractors should be responsible for the supervision and administration of all sub-contracts in accordance with the conditions of contract and should be responsible for the organisation and progression of all sub-contract work".

The University alleged an implied term requiring the contractors to inspect and supervise the work of sub-contractors, but in view of the express provision in the bill in my view there is no room, nor need, for such an implied term.

The question arises of whether contractors who have in breach of contract failed to supervise sub-contractors properly with the result that the sub-contractors have executed work badly or supplied defective materials are exempt in respect of latent defects discharged from liability by the architects' issue of a certificate under 27(e).

The only case cited to me in this connection was *Walters* v *Whessoe & Shell Refining Co Ltd* (1960) 6 BLR 23, in which Whessoe had agreed to indemnify and hold Shell free against all claims arising out of operations undertaken by Whessoe in pursuance of the contract between them. The Court of Appeal held that Shell could not obtain indemnity in respect of its own negligence.

Devlin LJ said at p 34: "It is now well established that if a person obtains an indemnity against the consequences of certain acts, the indemnity is not to be construed so as to include the consequences of his own negligence unless those consequences are covered directly or by necessary implication. They are covered by necessary implication if there is no other subject matter upon which the indemnity could operate. Like most rules of construction, this one depends upon the presumed intention of the parties".

Condition 27(e) does not create an indemnity, although, of course, it envisages the contractors obtaining one from the sub-contractors. So far as the employees and contractors are concerned, it is an exemption clause. Its proper construction must like the clause in *Whessoe* depend upon the presumed intention of the parties.

The reason for contractors being liable for the bad work of sub-contractors is because the contractors have themselves agreed under condition 1(1) to carry out the works to the satisfaction of the architects. This is so, even when the sub-contractors are nominated and are not of the contractors' selection. In substance, however, the position of the contractors in relation to the sub-contractors is not unlike that of vicarious liability which applies between employer and employee and of principal and agent in tort.

I think that the intention of the parties must be presumed to have been that condition 27(e) should exempt the contractors from liability in respect of the sub-contractors' failures, but not in connection with the contractors' personal breaches of contract. In my opinion, notwithstanding the issue of a certificate under the condition, contractors may still be liable for failure to supervise the sub-contractors and damages recoverable from them may take account of bad work which they should have detected.

Whether the works carried out by the contractors personally were in accordance with the contract drawings and bills as required by condition 1(1) and whether they were carried out in a good and workmanlike manner depends principally upon whether the reinforced concrete frames of phases I and II were within the tolerances laid down in the respective bills.

On phase II Mr Pochin agreed to pay £1 700 of the £12 700 eventually paid to the sub-contractors in respect of dubbing. That could be taken to be an admission that a little over 13 per cent of the dubbing was made necessary because of the structure being out of tolerance. Mr Pochin said, however, that at the time when he agreed to pay the £1 700, he believed, as I think everyone else did, that the tolerances were stricter than the experts agreed that they were. He said also that the payment was mainly with reference to the toilet ducts, which have figured little in the case.

The only direct evidence of deviation from tolerances related to parts of Crawford House and consisted of dimensions taken mainly with plant lines during the trial contract works in the winter of 1980–81 and the results of a laser survey of March 1982, each at least 10 years after the building was erected. The size of the alleged deviations was small by ordinary standards, for building can never be exact. Opinions differed as to whether Crawford House would have moved since it was built. I think that some movement has almost certainly occurred. Mr Pochin demonstrated how a change in datum for the laser survey could have produced different results and Mr Kinnear, who has had long experience of laser surveys, criticised the manner in which the March 1982 one was conducted.

From June 1969 onwards the architects, Mr Roper, the respective consultant engineers and the contractors were all concerned to ensure that the structure was built within tolerances and they all checked for line and level, rechecked and did not hesitate to condemn what they thought was unsatisfactory. Only concrete which had received general approval was allowed to stand. It is hard to believe that all concerned were wrong.

The amount of dubbing on phase II was much larger than that on phase I, but it was signed for by the clerk of works and, apart from the relatively small contribution made by the contractors, all was paid for by the University, with the approval of the architects.

I am left with the suspicion that parts of phase II and possibly parts of phase I were built out of tolerance, but I have to decide whether or nor they were, not on a basis of suspicion, but on a balance of probabilities. Applying that standard, the University has not in my opinion proved that the contractors erected the concrete frames out of tolerance, and therefore in breach of contract.

The position with regard to parapet walls is different. The concrete to form them was undoubtedly not taken up to the correct heights, so that extra dubbing was required before tiles were fixed. Sadly no one seems to have paid much attention to the achievement of correct levels of concrete in the walls; possibly because it was not kept sufficiently in mind that the tops of the walls would be tiled and grouted and would not be covered with a metal coping. I think that in the case of the gutter in the Booth Street elevation of Cornbrook House the lowness of the concrete and the bricks must have been deliberate and authorised.

The contractors' duty to warn the architects of defects which they believed existed in the architects' design did not, in my view, require them to make a critical survey of the drawings, bills and specifications, looking meticulously for mistakes. They should no doubt have obtained or at least read a copy of CP 212, but, even so, I do not think that they were under an obligation to decide passage by passage whether the architects had designed in accordance with it. Even in respect of the spacing of movement joints I think that they were entitled to assume that the architects in not following CP 212 knew what they were about. The contractors were employed principally to build and not to act as scrutineers of design.

I think that the contractors' obligation to warn arose when, in the light of their general knowledge and practical experience, they came to believe that an aspect of the design was wrong. As they had had no previous experience of external tiling, it is not surprising that they did not discover defects in the tiling design. Later, after the stains had appeared they believed that the choice of Fondu no 1 as grout was wrong and they said so. They also believed that the parapet wall design and the method of fixing the lightning conductor cable were wrong and again they said so. I am surprised that they did not criticise the window and skylight designs and the method of fixing the balustrades, but, since they made comments with regard to other matters, I infer that these did not occur to them. The architects did not welcome advice but appeared to resent it, which cannot have encouraged the contractors to proffer it.

I hold that the contractors did not act in breach of the implied term requiring them to give warning.

There was no positive evidence that the contractors obtained an indemnity from the sub-contractors in respect of latent defects before the architects issued their interim certificate under condition 27(e) releasing to the sub-contractors the retention monies in relation to phase I and the contractors parted with the money. However, I think that I may safely infer that they did so.

Before the interim certificate in respect of phase II was issued an indemnity was undoubtedly provided by the sub-contractors. It was not restricted to latent defects, but it included them. It was qualified to the extent that the sub-contractors had to be given the opportunity to rectify any defects before they could become financially liable for them.

I think that the indemnity was one within the contemplation of condition 27(e), but, in any event, since indemnities are solely for the benefit of contractors, I think that the contractors in this case could have limited their scope or even dispensed with them altogether if that was their wish.

Whether the contractors can escape what I will inaccurately but conveniently call vicarious liability for bad workmanship on the part of the sub-contractors must depend upon whether that bad workmanship gave rise to defects which were latent at the date of the certificates.

Applying as test whether the defects could have been discovered on such examination as a reasonably skilful man in the construction industry would have made I think the answer must be in the affirmative. The defects must be classed as patent. It follows that the certificates discharged the contractors from liability.

The contractors, because their staff were on site all the time, had greater opportunities for supervision of the sub-contractors than had the architects and as much or more than the clerk of works. Just as the architects and Mr Roper should have discovered the sub-contractors' failures and bad workmanship, so in my opinion should the contractors.

Failures to supervise properly was the contractors' personal failure. It follows that in my view condition 27(e) does not protect them. I hold that they acted in breach of contract.

The fourth issue is *whether the sub-contractors acted in breach of the direct warranty between the University and themselves in respect of phase II, in breach of the sub-contracts between the contractors and themselves in respect of phases I and II, and breach of duty in negligence to the University and, assuming for the present that such a duty exists, in breach of duty in negligence to the contractors.*

In have no doubt that the sub-contractors by failing to butter the backs of tiles properly, by leaving sand between some tile courses, by applying Bal-mix in greater thicknesses than ½ in and by not dubbing the concrete in parapet walls in layers acted in breaches of duty.

The fifth issue is *whether under the Law Reform (Contributory Negligence) Act 1945, the contractors are able to obtain a reduction in whatever is the amount of damages which they must pay by reason of contributory negligence of the University acting by their alter personae or agents, the architects, and/or their employee, the clerk of works?*

Section 1(1) of the Act of 1945 reads (omitting the provisos):

"Where any person suffers damage partly as the result of his own fault and partly of the fault of any other person or persons, a claim in respect of that damage shall not be defeated by reason of the fault of the persons suffering the damage, but the damage recoverable in respect thereof shall be reduced to such extent as the Court thinks just and equitable having regard to the claimant's share in the responsibility for the damage."

Section 4 assigns to the expression "fault" the meaning:

"Negligence, breach of statutory duty or other act or omission which gives rise to a liability in tort or would, apart from this Act, give rise to the defence of contributory negligence".

In *Basildon District Council* v *J. E. Lesser (Properties) Ltd (1984)* CILL 74 defendants, who had undertaken to indemnify the plaintiffs in respect of breaches of contract by contractors, responsible for certain aspects of design, sought to set up as contributory negligence the failure of the plaintiffs' architects' department to detect mistakes in the contractors' drawings.

After looking at passages in Halsbury's *Laws of England* (4th edition), Professor Glanville Williams' *Joint Torts and Contributory Negligence* and various other textbooks, and after reviewing as best I could the English and Commonwealth decisions, I came to the conclusions that contributory negligence had never been a defence in contract, that the Act of 1945 did not apply to contract and that, therefore, the defendants failed. In particular I followed the reasoning of Pritchard J in *Rowe* v *Turner Hopkins & Partners* [1980] 2 NZLR 530.

In this case Mr Garland accepted that prior to 1945 contributory negligence did not ordinarily apply to breach of contract, but he said that there was a "grey area", where a breach involved a failure to take care, where it might have applied. He relied principally upon *Caswell* v *Powell Duffryn Associated Collieries Ltd* [1940] AC 152, in which the House of Lords held that an action in respect of injuries caused by a breach of statutory duty did not differ from an action in respect of injuries caused by any other wrong and that contributory negligence could be relied upon as a defence to it.

Mr Garland said that in any event the description and uses of "fault" in the 1945 Act made the Act applicable to breaches of contract of types which were within the description. Mr Garland very persuasively and tactfully submitted that my decision in *Basildon* was wrong.

Mr Garland's arguments illustrated new facets of the question, but I am still of the view that the Act of 1945 does not apply to breach of contract. I will state my reaons briefly and without quoting afresh from the authorities which I referred to in *Basildon*:

(1) At common law, negligence as a basis of civil liability involved an element of fault, of blameworthiness, in that the defendant had acted carelessly.

(2) When the plaintiff had also been careless and therefore blameworthy,his conduct had to be brought into account, and if his carelessness operated at the same time as that of the defendant, the defendant would defeat his claim. There was no need for the plaintiff's carelessness to constitute a breach of duty to the defendant: it was sufficient that he had failed to take care of himself.

(3) The doctrine of contributory negligence was gradually applied to stricter, older forms, forms of liability in tort and it was natural to apply it to breach of statutory duty, when that was recognised as a cause of action and was invariably treated as part of tort.

(4) In contract blameworthiness was irrelevant. If a defendant had agreed under seal or for valuable consideration to do something, he had to do it, and if he failed he was liable, unless the obligation which the defendant had to fulfil itself required him to take care, whether he had done so or not was of no consequence. Carelessness on the part of the plaintiff in looking after himself could not affect his right to succeed against the defendant, although if it also constituted a breach of duty to the defendant in tort or contract it might in turn expose the plaintiff to an action by the defendant.

(5) The mischief which the 1945 Act was intended to mitigate was the harshness of the doctrine of contributory negligence to plaintiffs. The doctrine, and therefore the harshness, applied only in tort. It would have been a strange result of the Act if it had operated to introduce contributory negligence into contract for the benefit of defendants.

(6) The meaning of the Act is to be found primarily in its wording. It is to apply where a plaintiff has suffered because of his own fault and the defendant's fault. The description of fault is comprehensive; the first part of it is applicable to the defendant and the second part to the plaintiff. The first part is concerned with: Negligence – the most important nominate tort and also a method of committing many torts; with breach of statutory duty – part of tort, but probably mentioned specifically for the avoidance of doubt; and with "other act or omission which gives rise to a liability in tort", so incorporating all torts. The second part is unhappily expressed, because its linking with the first part could conceivably cause it to be read as meaning that only conduct sufficient to constitute a tort would suffice for contributory negligence, and that a duty has to be owed to the defendant, but it does at least underline the connection with tort. The last words, "give rise to the defence of contributory negligence", are clear; since at the

date of the Act contributory negligence applied only to tort, the Act was to apply to tort.

Because of the view which I take of the law I hold that the contractors cannot obtain any reduction in damages payable by them because of contributory negligence. If I had reached a different legal conclusion or if the University had not withdrawn their claim in negligence, I should have held that the failure of supervision by the architects as agents for the University and by the clerk of works, which I have found under issues 1 and 2, constituted contributory negligence by the University, resulting in a reduction in damages.

The sixth issue is *whether the contractors may by relying upon circuity of actions defeat the University's claims in respect of the concrete structure (assuming that I was wrong under issue 3 in holding that it was not proved) and in respect of the tiling (assuming that I was right in holding under issue 3 that because of their failure to supervise the sub-contractors properly they are liable for the sub-contractors' bad workmanship)*

A defence of circuity was not pleaded specifically, but facts giving rise to it were and it has been argued fully.

Circuity of actions as a defence would seem to have been forgotten for a long period after 1875, but it was clearly recognised by the Court of Appeal in *Post Office* v *Hampshire County Council* [1980] 1 QB 124, in which a claim by the Post Office against the County Council under the Telegraph Acts for damage to its underground cables was rejected because the Post Office had provided inaccurate information as to the cables' location. In *EDAC* I held that contractors who had unwittingly acted in breach of regulations and so of contract by complying with architects' contract drawings could rely on circuity, since they were entitled to be indemnified by the employers as principals of the architects.

Mr Garland contended that the architects and clerk of works, acting on behalf of the University, by failing to condemn concrete which was out of tolerance and by allowing the sub-contractors to proceed with tiling when they were not doing it properly, were setting standards which the contractors were entitled to assume indicated that the works were to the reasonable satisfaction of the architects within condition 1(1) of the contracts and were also in accordance with the requirements of the University.

In my opinion, if the architects and Mr Roper allowed concrete to remain which was not in accordance with tolerances, they were not thereby setting standards, but were simply failing to inspect and to supervise properly. The contractors contracted with the University to build according to the drawings and bills and, if they did not do so, they acted in breach of contract. The fact that the architects and clerk of works also failed to do their work properly and so failed to check them would not entitle the contractors to an indemnity and there is no room for a defence based on circuity of action. Similarly with the tiling.

The seventh issue is as to *the damages which the University may recover from the contractors for breaches of contract by them.*

I was helpfully reminded of cases beginning with *Robinson* v *Harman* (1848) Exch Rep. 850 and ending with *IBA* v *EMI* (1980) 14 BLR 1, House of Lords, setting out well established principles of law applicable to damages for breach of contract. Such damages are intended to compensate. Subject to two qualifications a plaintiff may recover all loss caused to him by the breach. The first qualification is that he must so far as possible have mitigated his loss and the second is that the loss must have been foreseeable at the time of the contract, otherwise it is too remote.

I was also referred to cases in which damages for the same loss was claimed from two or more contract-breakers. Among these cases were:

Burrows v *The March Gas and Coke Company* (1870) 5 Exchequer Cases 67, in which the defendants had laid a gas pipe in the plaintiffs' shop and, when a servant of a gasfitter went to investigate with a lighted candle, there was an explosion and the shop was destroyed. The court was uncertain whether the plaintiffs' action was in contract or in tort, but held that he could maintain it against both wrongdoers. Pigott B said at p 74: ". . . the mere fact of another cause having co-operated with the main cause does not make the main cause remote".

Heskell v *Continental Express Limited* [1950] 1 All ER 1033, in which among other events detention of goods and issue of a bill of lading by different persons had each contributed to loss sustained by the plaintiff.
Devlin J said at p 1048:

"Whatever the true rule of causation may be I am satisfied that if a breach of contract is one of two causes, both co-operating and both of equal efficacy . . . it is sufficient to carry judgment for damages".

Nowlan v *Brunswick Construction Ltd* (1972) 34 ALR (3D) 422 was a decision of the New Brunswick Supreme Court, Appeal Division, in which a house had developed dry rot, because its architect's design had failed to provide proper ventilation and its builder had failed among other things to provide a vapour barrier which was impervious to water.
Limerick J said at p 425:

"Where there are concurrent torts, concurrent breaches of contract or a breach of contract and a concurrent tort both contributing to the same damage, whether or not the damage would have occurred in the absence of either cause, the liability is a joint and several liability and either party causing or contributing to the damage is liable for the whole damage to the person aggrieved".

The learned judge relied upon *Thompson* v *LCC* [1899] 1 QB 840 (CA), which was however concerned with procedural rather than substantive matters. Limerick J was supported by the majority in the Supreme Court of Canada: (1974) 21 BLR 27.

It is surprising that there are not more cases, but I think that the law is clear: if two or more defendants have each committed breaches of the same or different contracts with the plaintiff and as the result of each defendant's breach the plaintiff has suffered the same damage he may recover the whole amount of it from any of the defendants.

The respects in which I have held that the contractors acted in breach of contract and what I think were the physical consequences of the breaches are as follows:

(1) Failing to build parapet walls to correct heights, so that more dubbing than would otherwise have been required had to be added to them. It may be that the extra dubbing should have been added in layers and have had reinforcement embedded in it, so as to create strong walls, but so far as water penetration is concerned, I do not think that how the dubbing was treated matters. Water which had passed through grout between tiles would have been able to penetrate either dubbing or concrete and so get behind tiles equally well.

(2) Failing to supervise the sub-contractors with sufficient care to prevent them leaving sand between courses to provide both an easy entrance for water and a storage place for it.

(3) Failing to supervise the sub-contractors, with sufficient care to ensure that they buttered the backs of the tiles properly and did not leave voids in which water could be held or through which it could percolate. Water behind tiles could in its normal form gradually break down the adhesion of Bal-mix to tiles or to dubbing or concrete, but as frost, or just conceivably as vapour, it could by its expansion have more immediate effects.

The respects in which I found under issue 1 that the architects acted in breach of contract and at the same time and in the same ways in breach of duty in tort to the University and what would I think have been the consequences of their breaches are as follows (not taking them in the same order as in issue 1):

(1) Designing parapet walls without metal copings, but clad with tiles, grouted with a non-waterproof grout, on their flat tops and sides so that water could enter easily and reach the backs of tiles on the walls and the face of the main concrete frame. Expecting Bal-mix to adhere to sand and cement slurry on top of asphalt.

(2) Requiring or permitting lightning conductors and balustrades to be fixed in such a manner as to penetrate tiles and provide ways for the admission of water.

(3) Designing windows so that water was likely to penetrate their surrounds and get behind tiles.

(4) Specifying Fondu no 1 grout knowing that it was not waterproof.

(5) Providing for such small gaps between tiles as to be difficult to grout, so that unsealed gaps were likely to be left.

(6) Failing to supervise the sub-contractors with sufficient care, so that in places they left sand between courses to provide entrance for water and to soak it up.

(7) Failing to supervise with sufficient care so as to ensure that the sub-contractors buttered the backs of tiles properly and did not leave voids to hold or provide ways for water.

(8) Permitting or failing to prevent the sub-contractors from using Bal-mix for combined adhesion and dubbing to a greater overall thickness than ½ in so weakening its adhesive strength.

(9) Using red tiles, so increasing the risk of thermal expansion and compressive stresses affecting adhesion.

(10) Providing for such small gaps between tiles as to increase risk of thermal and compressive action affecting adhesion.

(11) Designing for movement/expansion joints at 18 ft distances, when 10 ft would have been appropriate, and not providing for such joints where tiles in different planes met, so increasing risk of thermal and compressive action affecting adhesion.

(12) Failure to heed suggestions and advice with regard to Fondu no 1 grout, parapet walls, window surrounds and lightning conductors, so that errors continued. Failing generally to review their design.

(13) Designing on the basis of ceramic tiles when the University wanted a trouble free building of long life, Mr Thomas was apprehensive about their use, external use of tiles was relatively untried in Britain, the building was to be without features which would protect vertical surfaces, problems of tolerances were certain to arise and there were available alternatives to tiles, such as brick, metal sheeting and possibly fair-face weather-proof concrete, which would have met their water-proofing and aesthetic requirements. Contrary to the architects' belief tiles could never have lasted the life of the Centre, and by adopting a tiling solution the architects exposed the University to unnecessary risks.

Obviously the contractors and the architects committed some breaches of contract in common, but in my view the architects were guilty of many more and more extensive breaches than were the contractors. Nonetheless, if the damages resulting were the same the contractors would be liable for all. However, I do not think the damages were the same.

Leaving aside the concrete in the walls, the contractors' failure to prevent the sub-contractors from leaving sand between courses and to prevent the creation of voids behind the tiles made it possible for water action to bring about adhesion failures. The most, however, which can have stemmed from these breaches of contract is water action failure. The contractors' failure to supervise could not have caused thermal or compressive failures, which the architects' design had made inevitable. The responsibility for the University being provided with a building clad with tiles which were bound to require replacement after only a fraction of the life of the building was solely that of the architects.

If all had been well with parapet copings, window details, choice of grout, movement and expansion joints and the like, the tiles affected by water could have been replaced by new tiles properly buttered onto the concrete or dubbing, without any sand being left between tiles. *Prima facie*, therefore, I think that the University is entitled to recover from the contractors the cost of such an operation, at a date after they had come to know of failures on phase I as well as on phase II and had had an opportunity to consider the position. I think that about a year after Mr Crocker's first report, recommending a survey of phase I would be appropriate: say early 1980.

In fact, however, the defects in the tiling of the Centre were not confined to sand and voids and all the advice which the University received between 1979 and 1980 was to the effect that replacement of tiles would not prove a satisfactory solution and that another must be adopted. Sir Donald Gibson's proposals for use of textured cement was not practicable except on sheltered soffits and possibly columns, because the concrete was not waterproof and for reasons of appearance. What happened to metal sheeting at Warwick might well have happened at Manchester and there was also aesthetic reason for limiting the use of sheeting to the bridge, windows and tops of parapet walls.

I think that the University were fully justified in adopting a mainly brick solution, particularly as they first carried out a trial contract. The brick solution has the additional advantage that it avoids noisy and dirty operations, which would have been necessary to remove the surviving tiles and possibly some of the dubbing, but even without that advantage, I think that it was right.

Since retiling did not take place in 1980 and will never take place, the question arises of whether damages which resulted from the contractors' breaches of contract, to be estimated by the cost of retiling in 1980, are subsumed in the larger losses of the University, represented by the cost of the brick solution. Because the University had had to adopt the larger rather than the smaller solution, has it in the event suffered loss as the result of the contractors' breaches?

On general principle I think that the position in contract must be that when a defendant has agreed to make something for a plaintiff and has made it badly, the plaintiff is entitled to be compensated by receiving a sum which would enable him to have whatever it was made properly and it is irrelevant whether on completion it would be of use to him or not. It is equally unimportant whether the plaintiff intends actually to spend the money on that purpose.

I think, therefore, that the University may recover from the contractors the 1980 cost of retiling. The cost would be that of the work as required by the original drawings and specification and not on the basis of an improved specification: in other words in accordance with Mr Roberts' approach rather than that of Mr Seward. Unfortunately, Mr Roberts and Mr Seward did not consider what would have been their respective estimates adjusted for 1980.

If the retiling had been carried out in 1980, since presumably it would have been classed as repair and not as new work, it would have attracted Value Added Tax. However, the retiling was never carried out, but instead much more extensive work was executed, which the VAT Appeal Tribunal categorised as new. In the circumstances I do not think that any sum should be added on account of VAT, but I am conscious that the point has not been argued.

Failures in tiling due to water action would by themselves have necessitated the temporary closure of roads and pavements and the use of protective scaffolding and, therefore, I think that contractors should bear the whole of whatever costs were necessary on that account, but only up to say mid-1980. The contractors should also pay some part of the cost of the short-term remedial work, again up to 1980.

The contractors should bear the cost of additional dubbing on parapet walls made necessary by the concrete in them being too low. Possibly this figure can be calculated; if not then the University is entitled to nominal damages to mark the breach of contract.

The eighth issue is as to *the damages which the University may recover from the sub-contractors*.

I have already held under issue 4 that the sub-contractors acted in breach of a direct warranty agreement between themselves and the University in respect of phase II and in breach of duty and negligence in respect of both phases. The sub-contractors owed a duty in negligence because of the proximity of their relationship to the University; see *Junior Books* v *Veitchi Co Ltd* [1982] 3 All ER 201, to which I will refer more fully later.

The sub-contractors pleaded a Limitation Act defence against the University, but I think that the burden of proving it was upon them and, since they have not appeared to support it, I may disregard it.

It has not been proved that either the excessive thicknesses of Balmix or the wrong method of dubbing parapet walls caused any special damage. In other respects I think that the sub-contractors' liability to the University is the same as that of the contractors and in the same amount.

The ninth issue is *whether the architects are liable to the contractors in tort*.

If or when an architect employed by a building owner owes a duty to contractors and others has been considered by the courts in a number of cases.

In *Clayton* v *Woodman* (1962) 4 BLR 65 the Court of Appeal decided that an architect, who had refused to vary contract works which involved alterations to an existing building, was not liable to one of the contractor's workmen when a part of the building fell on him. Pearson LJ said at p 77:

> "The architect . . . is engaged as the agent of the owner . . . his function is to make sure that . . . when the work has been completed, the owner will have a building properly constructed in accordance with the contract . . . The architect does not undertake . . . to advise the builders as to what safety precautions should be taken or, in particular, as to how he should carry out his building operations".

In *Clay* v *A. J. Crump & Sons Ltd* [1964] 1 QB 533 the Court of Appeal held that architects employed to plan and supervise the redevelopment of a site who had allowed a defective wall to remain standing were liable to a contractor's workman upon whom it fell. Ormrod LJ after referring to *Donoghue* v *Stevenson* [1932] AC 562, said at p 556:

> "Is this a case in which it can be said that the plaintiff was so closely and directly affected by the acts of the architect as to have been reasonably in his contemplation when he was directing his mind to the acts or omissions which are called in question? In my judgment there must be an affirmative answer to that question. The architect, by reason of his contractual arrangement with the building owner, was charged with the duty of preparing the necessary plans and making arrangements for the manner in which the work should be done. This involved taking precautions or giving instructions for them to be taken so that the work could be done with safety. It must have been in the contemplation of the architect that builders would go on the site as the whole object of the work was to erect buildings thereon. It would seem impossible to contend that the plantiff would not be affected by the decisions and plans drawn up by the architect".

In *Oldschool* v *Gleeson (Contractors) Limited* (1976) 4 BLR 103 contractors, who had admitted liability to employers, sought indemnity or contributions from architects but they failed. Judge Stabb QC, Official Referee, after quoting from Pearson LJ in *Clayton's* case said *obiter* at p 131:

> ". . . it seems abundantly plain that the duty of care of an architect or of a consulting engineer in no way extends into the area of how the work is carried out. Not only has he no duty to instruct the

builder how to do the work or what safety precautions to take but he has no right to do so, nor is he under a duty to the builder to defect faults during the progress of the work. The architect, in that respect, may be in breach of duty to his client, the building owner, but this does not excuse the builder from faulty work.

I take the view that the duty of care which an architect or a consulting engineer owes to a third party is limited by the assumption that the contractor who executes the works acts at all times as a competent contractor. The contractor cannot seek to pass the blame for incompetent work on to the consulting engineer on the ground that he failed to intervene to prevent it".

In *Sutcliffe* v *Thackrah* [1974] AC 727 the House of Lords held that in issuing a Certificate an architect is not acting as an arbitrator. In *Arenson* v *Arenson* [1977] AC 405, a case concerned with a valuer, Lord Salmon said at p 438 when referring to *Sutcliffe:*

"The architect owed a duty to his client, the building owner, arising out of the Contract between them to use reasonable care in issuing his Certificate. He also, however, owed a similar duty of care to the Contractor arising out of their proximity".

In *Junior Books Ltd* v *Veitchi Co Ltd* [1982] 3 All ER 201, a case which was not concerned with an architect and contractors, but with an employer and sub-contractors, the House of Lords held that there was sufficient proximity between them for it to be possible for the sub-contractors to have owed a duty of care to the employer when laying a floor not to create economic loss.

I think that in view of the House of Lords cases Judge Stabb's words in *Oldschool* must now be regarded as too widely expressed. Because of proximity an architect may sometimes owe a duty of care to contractors even in relation to how they carry out their work. If, for example, an architect knew that on a site with which they were concerned contractors or sub-contractors were making a major mistake which would involve the contractors in expense, I think that the architect would probably owe a duty to the contractors to warn them. In those circumstances the architect would not be instructing the contractors in how to do their work, but merely warning them of the probable consequences of persistence in the particular method which they had adopted.

In this case, however, the architects clearly did not discover that the sub-contractors were doing or had done their work badly. They had no knowledge which they could communicate. They knew that the contractors were themselves under an express duty to inspect the sub-contractors' work and had no reason to believe that the contractors would not inspect properly. In all the circumstances I conclude that the architects did not owe the contractors a duty to exercise when inspecting. It follows that the architects were not in breach of duty to the contractors.

The architects were, as I have held under issue 1, in breach of duty to the University by failing to inspect properly and if the University had not, consequent upon their agreement with the architects, withdrawn their claim against the contractors in tort, I should unhesitatingly have made orders for apportionment between them under the Law Reform (Married Women and Tortfeasors) Act 1935.

The tenth and final issue is *whether the sub-contractors are liable to the contractors in contract or in tort.*

The sub-contractors acted in breach of their contract with the contractors. Because of proximity they also owed a duty of care to the contractors in tort and by fixing the tiles as they did acted in breach of it. The sub-contractors did not plead any defence based on provisions of the sub-contracts, but they set up the Limitation Act, which, as I said before under issue 8, I disregard. I order the sub-contractors to indemnify the contractors in respect of the whole amount which they have to pay to the University, except for that payable in relation to the parapet walls.

In conclusion, unfortunately I am not able to give judgment immediately in money terms because of the uncertainties as to figures which I have mentioned under issue 7. There are also questions of interest and of costs to be determined. When dealing with them I can deal with the contractors' set-off or counterclaim which has not hitherto been the subject of consideration. Unless the parties agree these matters there will have to be an adjourned hearing.

Even though the case is incomplete I must thank counsel and solicitors for the way in which it has been presented. If proofs had not been exchanged, experts had not met and if counsel had not supplied notes of their submissions, the trial must have lasted very much longer and I should have found grappling with its many aspects and complexities even more taxing!

COUNSEL

For the University: Mr Brian Knight QC and Mr R. Wilmot-Smith (instructed by Messrs Addleshaw Sons and Latham).
For Hugh Wilson: Mr Michael Wright QC and Mr R. Ter Haar (instructed by Messrs Kennedys).
For Pochin (Contractors) Ltd: Mr P. Garland QC and Mr C. Thomas (instructed by Messrs Grundy Kershaw & Bowdens).

Building contract JCT Minor Works form – Architect's certificate –
Whether court has power to open up and review architect's certificates
and opinions

ORAM BUILDERS LTD   Plaintiffs

v

M. J. PEMBERTON & C. PEMBERTON   Defendants

Queen's Bench Division
(Official Referees' Business)
1 February 1985

His Honour Judge
David Smout QC

Where there is an arbitration clause in general terms in a building contract, the court has no power to open up, review and revise the architect's certificates and opinions

The plaintiffs (building contractors) entered into a contract with the defendants dated 14 July 1982. The contract was in the JCT Agreement for Minor Building Works form (1980 edition, October 1981 revision), article 4 of which is an arbitration agreement in general terms. Clause 3.6 of the contract empowers the architect/supervising officer to order variations. The supervising officer issued instructions to the plaintiffs which constituted a substantial variation of the contract. The plaintiffs claimed to have done the extra work so required and sought a certificate for its payment. This was not forthcoming and the plaintiffs claimed the extra cost of the extra work, or alternatively damages. The defendants disputed the plaintiffs' claim and counterclaimed for alleged breaches of contract. The preliminary issue, with which this judgment is concerned, was whether the court had power to review the exercise of the supervising officer's discretionary power under the contract and open up his certificates.

HELD: The court has no jurisdiction to go behind a certificate of the architect/supervising officer. "Where there is an arbitration clause in general terms referring any dispute or difference between the parties concerning the contract to the arbitrator . . . then even on a narrow interpretation of the reasoning of the Court of Appeal in *Northern Regional Health Authority* v *Derek Crouch Construction Co Ltd* [1984] QB 644; [1984] 2 All ER 175, the High Court has no jurisdiction to go behind" an architect's certificate.

HIS HONOUR JUDGE DAVID SMOUT QC: This is an interlocutory application seeking the court's ruling on the matter of jurisdiction. The parties wish the court to review certain decisions of the supervising officer appointed under the particular variant of the standard JCT form of contract which is appropriate for Minor Building Works.

The plaintiffs are building contractors who entered into such an agreement with the defendants on 14 July 1982. It was the 1980 edition reprinted with corrections in October 1981. Condition 3.6 provides that the supervising officer might, without invalidating the contract, order additional works, and it adds in effect that works done in accordance with such instructions are to be valued by the supervising officer on a fair and reasonable basis.

The supervising officer issued instructions to the plaintiffs which constituted a substantial variation of the contract. The plaintiffs claimed to have done the extra work so required and accordingly requested a certificate for payment for such extra work from the supervising officer. No such certificate was forthcoming. Thereupon the plaintiffs claimed the cost of such extra work from the defendants despite the absence of the certificate. The plaintiffs were not paid in that regard. The defendants terminated the contract for reasons which I need not go into at this stage. The plaintiffs by these proceedings seek to recover the alleged cost of the extra work, alternatively damages. It is common ground that quite apart from any extra work, the supervising officer did certify for some £63 000 which has been paid. The balance which the plaintiffs claim to be due is in excess of a further £52 000. The defendants whilst admitting the agreement denied the plaintiffs' claim and allege *inter alia* that the work which was done was of less value that that for which the supervising officer had certified and for which payment had already been made. They alleged moreover various breaches of contract by the plaintiffs and counterclaim for a sum in excess of £62 000.

It is apparent that if the various matters in dispute are to be resolved then that will necessitate opening up the certificates issued by the supervising officer and reviewing the exercise of his discretionary powers under the agreement.

Article 4 of the agreement contains an arbitration clause. It is in general terms as follows:

"If any dispute or difference concerning this Contract shall arise between the Employer or the Architect/Supervising Officer on his

behalf and the Contractor such dispute shall be and is hereby
referred to the arbitration and final decision of a person to be agreed
between the parties . . ."

By summons the defendants now ask the court to determine whether it
has jurisdiction to decide the matters in dispute. The parties both wish to
know where they stand in this regard at this stage rather than proceed to
trial and risk the jurisdiction point being taken either then or subsequently on appeal. In short the question is whether the guidance of the Court
of Appeal provided in *Northern Regional Health Authority* v *Derek Crouch Construction Co Ltd* [1984] QB 644 is as applicable in this respect to the JCT
Form of Agreement for Minor Building Works as it is to the JCT main
contract. In *Crouch* the Court of Appeal was directly concerned with the
powers of the High Court when determining the rights of parties under a
JCT main contract. The Court of Appeal determined that the High Court
had no power to review the architect's decisions in which were included
certificates, opinions, requirements and notices. Those powers were by
clause 35(3) of the JCT main contract expressly given to the arbitrator.
Clause 35(3) of the JCT main contract is the arbitration clause: it reads in
full:

> "Subject to the provisions of Clauses 2(ii), 30(vii) and 31D(iii) of
> these conditions the arbitrator shall, without prejudice to the gen-
> erality of his powers, have power to direct such measurements
> and/or valuations as may in his opinion be desirable in order to
> determine the rights of the parties and to ascertain and award any
> sum which ought to have been the subject of or included in any
> Certificate and to open up, review and revise any Certificate, Opin-
> ion, Decision, Requirement or Notice and to determine all matters
> in dispute which shall be submitted to him in the same manner as if
> no such Certificate, Opinion, Decision, Requirement or Notice had
> been given".

The guidance of the Court of Appeal in *Crouch* is to be found in the passages of the judgments of Dunn LJ at p 633D–664F, of Browne-
Wilkinson LJ at p 666G–668G, and of Sir John Donaldson MR at
p 670C–673F and 674H–675B. The following passage from the
judgment of Dunn LJ at p 644D–E is representative:

> "The contract gives the architect wide discretionary powers as to
> the supervision, evaluation and progress of the works. The parties
> have agreed that disputes as to anything left to the discretion of the
> architects should be referred to arbitration, and clause 35 gives wide
> powers to the arbitrator to review the exercise of the architect's
> discretion and to substitute his own views for those of the architect.
> Where parties have agreed on machinery of that kind for the resolu-
> tion of disputes, it is not for the court to intervene and replace its own
> process for the contractual machinery agreed by the parties".

As the Master of the Rolls indicated at p 675A the decision must extend beyond clause 35(2) to "its equivalent in other standard forms of contract". I do not conclude from the reasoning of the Court of Appeal, however, that it was the precise wording of clause 35 that was decisive in this respect. Both Dunn LJ and the Master of the Rolls cited the dictum of Lord Wilberforce in *Hosier & Dickinson Ltd* v *P. & M. Kaye Ltd* [1972] 1 WLR 146 at p 158:

> "Had the matter gone to arbitration the position would no doubt have been different: this is because clause 35 of the contract confers very wide powers upon arbitrators to open up and review certificates which a Court would not have".

Browne-Wilkinson LJ at p 667B–D remarked:

> "In principle, in an action based on contract the court can only enforce the agreement between the parties: it has no power to modify that agreement in any way. Therefore, if the parties have agreed on a specified machinery for establishing their obligations, the court cannot substitute a different machinery. So, in this contract the parties have agreed that certain rights and obligations are to be determined by the certificate or opinion of the architect. In an action questioning the validity of an architect's certificates or opinion given or expressed under Clauses 22 or 23 of the main contract, in my judgment the Court's jurisdiction would be limited to deciding whether or not the certificate or opinion was legally invalid because given, for example, in bad faith or in excess of his powers. In no circumstances would the Court have power to revise such certificate or opinion solely on the ground that the court would have reached a different conclusion since so to do would be to interfere with the agreement of the parties".

As I understand it, the Court of Appeal was accordingly of the opinion not that the arbitration clause deprived the court of jurisdiction but rather that it gave to the arbitrator a jurisdiction to open up and review certificates which the court does not possess. On that interpretation it appears that whether or not there is any arbitration clause the court cannot go behind an architect's certificate. However, I do not have to go that far in the instant case. I am satisfied that where there is an arbitration clause in general terms referring any dispute or difference between the parties concerning the contract to the arbitrator – such as arises in the instant case – then even on a narrow interpretation of the reasoning of the Court of Appeal in *Crouch*, the High Court has no jurisdiction to go behind a certificate of an architect or supervising officer.

I recognise that an earlier Court of Appeal decision in *Neale* v *Richardson* [1938] 1 All ER 753 remains authority for the proposition that where there has been a failure of an architect to issue a certificate that is ordinarily a prerequisite for payment, then if the architect be the arbitrator under the contract and yet declines the arbitration, the court regains jurisdiction. In those limited circumstances the court is able to determine the rights of the parties in the absence of a certificate, but that is a thousand miles from this case.

There is a further aspect that should be mentioned. Even if the parties were to wish it, this is not a case where the court could properly try some issues and leave others to arbitration. One can visualise difficulties wherever such a procedure were to be adopted; not least because there are different provisions in respect of appeal from an arbitrator than that from an Official Referee. In the instant case such a procedure is wholly unrealistic. This dispute involves investigations of allegations on the one side of underpayment and on the other of overpayment for work done. It must be taken as a whole. Yet the court is incapable of determining it as a whole for it cannot look where it matters, namely, behind the supervising officer's certificates and opinions.

The lack of jurisdiction is not cured merely by the parties' expressed preference for litigation. Neither is it of any consequence that steps in the action were taken by both parties after the decision of the Court of Appeal in *Crouch* was handed down. This is not a matter of election or even of estoppel. Such steps cannot confer on the High Court a jursidiction which, it is now known, never did exist. If as has been suggested the parties still desire the dispute as a whole to be determined by an Official Referee they must enter into an arbitration agreement in writing to that effect. In this particular instance, I am persuaded that such a course may well be expedient for the parties, bearing in mind that the pleadings were closed some time ago and much expense has already been incurred. Section 11 of the Arbitration Act, 1950 and RSC order 36, rule 5 (ii) are in point. The Official Referee would then have the powers of an arbitrator under article 4 of the contract and not the powers of the High Court judge.

For the moment it is enough for me to say that the High Court has not the jurisdiction to determine the issues that are set out in the pleadings. The parties will now wish to reconsider their position. Meanwhile I make no further order at this stage save to give liberty to apply.

COUNSEL
For the plaintiffs: Mr P. V. Boulding (instructed by Messrs Stringer, Saul & Justice).
For the defendants: Mr D. N. Sharpe (instructed by Messrs Montlake & Co).

Building regulations 1976 – Non-compliance with regulations – Duty of local authority to building owner – Whether building owner vicariously liable for negligence of architect – Whether building owner who is also experienced developer in different position from ordinary building owner – Whether architect entitled to rely on consulting engineer appointed to design and supervise foundations

ANGLIA COMMERCIAL PROPERTIES LTD

Plaintiffs

v

SOUTH BEDFORDSHIRE DISTRICT COUNCIL AND OTHERS

Defendants

Third parties

Queen's Bench Division
(Official Referees' Business)
27, 28 February, 1 March, 5, 6, 7, 8 March,
5 April 1984

His Honour Judge
Sir William Stabb QC

A building owner is not under an absolute non-delegable duty under the Building Regulations such as to render him liable for the negligence of his independent contractors.

Anglia, a property developer, claimed damages from the defendant local authority for negligence and/or breach of statutory duty as the authority responsible for approving site plans and in particular those for the foundations of four warehouses erected for Anglia on the site of a disused sandpit, which had at one time contained a large and deep pool of water. The claim arose out of the rapid disintegration and subsequent demolition of the four warehouses which had been erected on the site. The failure was due to the inadequate design of the foundations, having regard to the nature of the ground. The local authority contended that, as building owner, Anglia was itself under a duty to comply with the Building Regulations, and that this was a duty which could not be delegated to others such as Anglia's architects and consultant engineers, for whose negligence Anglia would, in any event, be vicariously liable. The local authority further contended that it was under no duty of care towards Anglia whom they alleged to be in breach of statutory duty and itself negligent or vicariously liable for the negligence of its architects or engineers.

HELD: Anglia was not under a non-delegable duty as contended, nor was Anglia itself negligent personally or vicariously. Judgment was given for Anglia on the claim against the local authority.

HIS HONOUR JUDGE SIR WILLIAM STABB QC: I have listened to four independent experts, expressing their respective views, and I think that it would be fair to say that they all agreed that where building work is to be carried out on made ground or fill, such as this ground was known to be, prudence demands that an investigation of the nature of the ground should be carried out in order to determine how the foundations should be designed so as to comply with the Building Regulations. Regulation D3 requires that a foundation of a building should safely sustain and transmit to the ground the imposed load in such a manner as not to cause any settlement which would impair the stability of the building. Regulation D4 provides that the requirements of Regulation D3 shall be deemed to be satisfied if the foundations are constructed in accordance with CP 2004. I need only refer to two parts of that Code of Practice, clause 2.2.2.2.2, table I, assigns no presumed bearing value to made ground or fill, and clause 2.2.2.3.5 provides that all made ground should be treated as suspect, because of the likelihood of extreme variability, and that any proposal to found a structure on made ground should be investigated with extreme care, and warns that loading tests may be completely misleading because of the variability of what might have been deposited in the fill. In this case the foundation design of the engineers which was passed by the local authority and specifically approved by the building inspector on site when excavation took place was a foundation for each portal frame consisting of a $6 \times 3 \times 3$ ft deep concrete block based upon a lean mix of concrete at a depth at which the engineers and the building inspector decided that the bottom was capable of providing a safe bearing pressure of 1 ton per ft^2 which was, as they thought, at a depth of approximately 6 ft in each case. As I have already stated, when the ground investigation was subsequently carried out, the depth of the fill was found to be 30 to 40 ft and with a high ratio of voids. I accept that it was the duty of the engineers to decide what site investigation should be carried out where, as here, it was known that the site was on made ground. I also accept that the only possible way of investigating the nature of the ground was by means of bore holes and subsequent laboratory analysis of the undisturbed samples. The digging of trial holes was quite useless. The engineers were at fault in failing to see that a proper investigation was carried out. Instead of this, they seem to have accepted the foundation sub-contractor's statement that virgin ground had been reached, which clearly was not the case, and they accordingly designed the simplest foundation which would have been suitable only for good intact clay. The engineers were clearly at fault, but the proceedings against them have been discontinued because they are uninsured. I am told that they have made a contribution of £10 000 towards the plaintiffs' costs.

So far as the local authority are concerned it was their statutory duty under s 64 of the Public Health Act 1936 to pass the plans if they complied with the regulations or to reject them if they did not. They gave building regulation approval at a time when they had not got the engineers' detailed design or calculations, and when they did subsequently receive them they should not have passed them, because they should have known that the required bearing pressure of 1 ton per ft^2 would not be accepted for what they, of all people concerned, should have known to be made ground or fill.

The building inspector, their servant and for whose acts they are responsible, was also at fault in giving his approval for each excavated base. True he may not have had the expertise to give any worthwhile judgment, but the local authority seem to have accepted that they with the engineers were to be the arbiters of when the bottom of each excavation was to be regarded as providing a base to provide the required bearing pressure, and thus involved themselves as judges of what was suitable, quite apart from their statutory duties in connection with the granting or refusing of building regulation approval.

It is small wonder that Mr Akroyd who was the independent consulting engineer called on behalf of the local authority, branded everyone concerned with this project as crazy. By saying that, he may have been casting his net too widely, but where a professionally qualified engineer, who is presumed to know the Building Regulations and the Codes of Practice and whose responsibility it is to design suitable foundations for a building which he must have known or should have found out was to be erected on a vast depth of fill, designs simple foundations suitable only for use on good intact clay, it is difficult to quarrel with Mr Akroyd's description. It is equally difficult to understand how the local authority, who were in a better position than any of the others to know the history of this site and the nature of the ground with which they were dealing, could have allowed these plans to pass or could have expressed their positive satisfaction with the bases excavated without having satisfied themselves at least that a soil investigation report had in some way confirmed or corroborated the validity of the design which

the engineers were submitting. It seems to me to be plain beyond per-
adventure that not only the engineers but also the local authority were
at fault. The engineers were in breach of contract and in breach of duty
to their clients, Anglia. The local authority owed a duty of care to
Anglia, even though Anglia were not the occupiers of the buildings and
even though they, as the building owners, engaged independent contractors to build and to design. This was established in *Acrecrest Ltd* v *W.
S. Hattrell & Partners* [1983] QB 260.

I hold that the local authority were in breach of their statutory duty
and in breach of their duty of care, and that these breaches were causa-
tive of the damage which Anglia have suffered as a result of the necessity to demolish and rebuild the two warehouses.

So far as the architect's role in all this is concerned, it is suggested
that because they must have known the nature of the site from the out-
set and because, when initially acting for [an earlier owner of the site
from whom Anglia purchased it] they envisaged poor ground conditions and suspected that piling might be necessary, they ought to
have realised that the foundations designed by the engineers would not
be suitable and that they should presumably have queried or objected
to the design. I have heard the evidence of Mr Robert Foster, FRIBA
and for many years a member of the Council of the Institute, and
formerly senior partner of his firm but now recently retired. He drew my
attention to the relevant clause of the Conditions of Engagement in use
at the time. It is clause 1.22 and reads as follows:

"The architect will advise on the need for independent consultants
and will be responsible for the direction and integration of their
work, but not for the detailed design, inspection and performance
of the work entrusted to them".

By that clause, I should have thought that the architects who had certainly advised on the necessity for engaging consulting engineers to
design the foundations were absolved from responsibility for the design
of the foundations, and that was Mr Foster's view. But it is interesting
to look at the clause currently in force. It was introduced in 1982 and
reads as follows:

"Where the client employs the Consultants [which in this case
Anglia certainly did] the client will hold each Consultant and not
the architect responsible for the competence general inspection
and performance of the work entrusted to that Consultant".

I think that this reflects, in clearer terms, what had been the position
under the previous conditions. It was interesting to hear Mr Winders,
himself a consulting engineer, state in evidence that in his view the
responsibility for the foundations was that of the engineers, upon whom
the architects were entitled to rely. He said that it was the duty of the
engineers to decide what site investigation should be carried out and he

had no doubt that in this instance the engineers should have ordered an investigation and were at fault in not so doing.

In the light of this evidence, I am satisfied that the architects, once the engineers had been appointed to design and supervise the foundations of these buildings, were entitled to rely upon the engineers' judgment as to what was suitable. They invited them to send the necessary structural information in support of the application for building regulation approval direct to the local authority, and in the result building regulation approval was given.

Whatever the risk presented by the nature of the ground, I think that the architects properly met that risk by seeing that consulting engineers were appointed to deal with it, and in those circumstances I acquit the architects of any responsibility for the failure of the foundations.

That leaves what I conceive to be the real issue in this case, namely the contention advanced on behalf of the local authority that Anglia were negligent themselves or through their architects and engineers for whose negligence they are vicariously liable or that Anglia were under an absolute non-delegable statutory duty to comply with the Building Regulations and because they were themselves negligent or in breach of statutory duty they cannot recover against the local authority because they are the source of their own loss or at least have contributed in part to it.

Dealing first with the allegation of contributory negligence, Mr Kidwell on behalf of Anglia has reminded me that contributory negligence is properly described as some act or omission on the plaintiff's part of such a nature that it may properly be described as negligence, only in the sense of careless conduct. It does not mean breach of any duty. The burden of proving contributory negligence is of course on the defendants and it is for them to establish that the plaintiff's contributory negligence was a substantial or material co-operating cause. It is a failure to use reasonable care so that the plaintiff becomes, at least partially the author of his own wrong. Mr Owen on behalf of the local authority contends that Anglia are developers and therefore one would expect them to have a measure of in-house expertise. He says that they must have known the nature of the site and of the existence of the fill: and when considering the purchase of the site in June 1972 Mr Mabey, a director of Anglia, wrote to the architects expressing interest in its purchase and said "I'll do my sums": that is to say presumably that he would work out the cost of the site and of the buildings that were to be erected on it and also the income which those buildings could be expected to produce in order to see whether it was likely to be a profitable project. Prudence he says required them to ask for a ground investigation without which they must have known that they were taking a risk in assessing the cost without knowing all that was involved. It seems to me that in order to meet that risk Anglia engaged a professional team, all of whom, with the approval of the local authority, accepted what is now clear were inadequate foundations. But it is said that it is the developers' duty to question the advice which their professional advisers gave them and that anyone with experience in the building industry should know of the problems posed by infill on a site on which buildings are to be erected and should know how to deal with those problems; be he architect, engineer, local authority, specialist sub-contractor or developer. I decline to equate a building owner, be he developer or otherwise, with his professional team in this way. In my view, he engages a professional team for the very purpose of being advised as to the right course to adopt. If there was any evidence to the effect that Anglia had refused to adopt or accept the advice of their architects or engineers to have a ground investigation, it might have been a different matter, but I cannot find any evidence to support such a suggestion. Everything points to the contrary. It is said that anyone should know that, where a site is on made ground or fill, a ground investigation is essential. I find this difficult to accept where the local authority, as here, with professionally qualified surveryor and engi-neer, still went on without such an investigation, and there could be no possible suggestion that Anglia were disgregarding their advice.

If the local authority acted as they did, I cannot understand how it can be said that Anglia should have known better. I conclude that the local authority have failed to establish that Anglia were themselves negligent.

If, as I believe, Anglia were not themselves negligent, they can only have been guilty of contributory negligence if vicariously liable for the negligence of others, those others being their professional team. But they are all independent contractors and employers are not liable for the negligent acts or omissions of an independent contractor except in certain limited circumstances, the only one of which in this instance is relied upon is where by statute an absolute duty is laid upon the employer. In those circumstances, the duty is a primary one and there-fore cannot be delegated, and if the employer seeks to assign the discharge of that duty to an independent contractor who fails to discharge it properly, the employer nevertheless remains liable. Here it is said that Anglia are under an absolute duty to comply with the Building Regulations, and that they cannot escape liability for breach of that duty if they have engaged a professional team and entrust to them the task of complying with the Building Regulations, even though the reason for engaging them was because they have the expertise to ensure compliance with the Building Regulations whereas Anglia have not. The duty, it is said, is absolute and owed to the world at large on the principle that by causing a building to be built which does not comply with the Building Regulations, they are, so to speak, putting on the market something which is potentially not safe and for which they should therefore be responsible. That was the view that was expressed by the Court of Appeal in New Zealand in the case of *Mount Albert Borough Council v Johnson* [1979] 2 NZLR 234. I think that it is fair to say that no English Court has travelled as far as to reach that conclusion. I am bound to say that I take the view that a building owner at least, in contrast to an owner-builder, is not under any non-delegable or absolute duty to comply with the Building Regulations and, indeed, may well not be under any statutory duty at all. The Building Regulations unhappily make no provision as to whose duty it should be to comply with this or that regulation. Regulation A10 provides that any person who intends to carry out what I summarize as a building operation must give notice to the local authority and deposit plans. It does not specify that those plans must comply with the Building Regulations, but if they do not, no doubt they will be rejected by the local authority, if the local authority comply with their statutory duty. Regulation A11, which deals with the giving of notices of the commencement and completion of stages of work by the builder, defines the builder as any person carrying out or intending to carry out the building operation referred to in Regulation A10. From a reading of these two regulations in juxtaposition there is some ground for thinking, therefore, that the only person concerned in those Building Regulations is the builder, and that unless the owner or the architect or anyone else deliberately intervenes to cause a non-compliance with the regulations, the person responsible for contravention is the builder. But it seems to me to be unnecessary to decide whether Anglia were or were not under a statutory duty to comply with the Building Regulations because I am quite satisfied that any such duty, if it existed, was not of the absolute non-delegable type of duty so as to leave them liable in the event of a breach of the regulations having been caused by the fault of an independent contractor. If such were the case, it seems to me that no building owner could prosecute any claim involving a breach of the Building Regulations, since it would immediately evoke the response that the building owner himself was responsible for the breach, and no such response, in my experience, has been evoked in those circumstances.

The question arose in the case of *Acrecrest Ltd v W. S. Hattrell & Partners* above cited and Stephenson LJ was content to base his decision on the assumption that such a statutory duty rested upon the building owner, but concluded that even in that event the local authority owed a duty of care to the building owner, which can only mean that the building owner, although under a statutory duty to comply with the Building Regulations, is still entitled to prosecute a claim against a local authority that has been at fault. At page 272 he said this:

"The local authority contended that the plaintiffs' failure to comply with the building regulations constitutes the negligence and guilt necessary to exclude them and they are in this respect no better off than the owner builder. To that the plaintiffs reply that unlike the owner-builder the duty to comply with the relevant Building Regulation is not imposed on them but on the builder. Assuming, as I have said that I shall assume for the purpose of this appeal, that the duty to comply with regulation D3(b) of the Building Regulations 1965 may rest upon the building owner who employs a builder and an architect as well as upon the builder, the plaintiffs are not, in my judgment, excluded from the duty owed by the local authority.

Again I base my decision on the language of Lord Wilberforce. He excludes a negligent building owner, not a building owner in breach of statutory duty, a negligent building owner who is the source of his own loss, not a building owner who is in breach of a statutory duty which he has relied on a competent builder to perform under the supervision of an architect and to some extent of the local authority's inspector. I would not describe such a building owner as either negligent or so negligent as to be the source of his own loss, and therefore unable to recover from any of those who are obviously negligent and responsible for the damage caused him, any contribution towards it. That is the kind of building owner to whom Lord Wilberforce's words indirectly refer and they do not catch the plaintiffs. They would, in my judgment, catch a building owner who, knowing the requirements of the inspector or of the building regulations, chooses to flout them."

And again on page 273 he said that:

"But in my judgment the original building owner can properly rely on his architect and builder to design and erect buildings which are not defective through want of reasonable care and skill or through failure to comply with building regulations or the local authority's instructions; and he does not, by employing them as independent contractors, remove himself from the class of those who are reasonably likely to be directly affected by the local authority's negligence or breach of statutory duty.

Developers in the plaintiffs' position are therefore in a relationship to the local authority in which a *prima facie* duty of care arises and the question is "whether there are any considerations which ought to negative or to reduce or limit the scope of the duty or the class of person to whom it is owed or the damages to which a breach of it may give rise" so as to exclude them or the damages arising from their having to repair the damage to these flats or compensating their lessees: see the classic statement of Lord Wilberforce in *Anns* v *Merton London Borough Council* [1978] AC728 at pp 751–752. I can find no consideration which excludes the plaintiffs from recovering these damages from the local authority and the local authority are consequently tortfeasors liable in respect of them."

In his judgment at page 282 Sir David Cairns set out the grounds of appeal relied on at the hearing. So far as this point is concerned he said this:

"This local authority's main contentions may be summarized as follows.
1. The local authority owed no duty of care to the plaintiffs (b) because the plaintiffs were themselves in breach of statutory duty under the Building Regulations 1965. (c) Because the negligence of their architects was attributable to them".

In dealing with those contentions later in his judgment Sir David Cairns said this:

"In my judgment all these contentions fail for the following reasons:
1(b) Assuming that a building owner who is not himself the builder is in breach of building regulations when his builder infringes them, I cannot accept that this excludes him from the category of persons to whom the duty of care is owed. It is obvious that the building owner will often in practice be ignorant of the provisions of the Building Regulations and will quite properly leave it to others to see that the regulations are complied with. Unless he was actually conscious that the work was being done illegally, he could not sensibly be regarded as one who was 'a negligent building owner the source of his own loss'.
1(c) There is no good reason why the negligence of architects, who are independent contractors, should be attributed to the building owners."

From these passages I think that it is clear that the court in that case was deciding that:
(1) Assuming that the building owner was under a statutory duty to comply with the Building Regulations, a breach of those regulations does not exclude the building owner from the class of persons to whom the local authority owes a duty of care.
(2) A building owner who has been put in breach through no fault of his own is not a negligent building owner the source of his own loss.
(3) The negligence of the contractors, the architects or the engineers, that is to say the professional team, who are independent contractors, is not to be attributed to the building owner.

From this, I conclude that if Anglia were under any statutory duty, it was not of the absolute non-delegable type which would render them liable for the negligence of their independent contractors, and as they were not themselves negligent, the defendants' allegation of contributory negligence must fail.

In the result I give judgment for the plaintiffs on the claim.

COUNSEL

For the plaintiff: R. Kidwell QC and A. Pugh (instructed by Messrs Hunt & Hunt, Romford).

For the defendant: J. Owen QC and A. Brunner (instructed by Messrs Barlow, Lyde & Gilbert).

For the second third party: H. Delotbinière (instructed by Messrs Mextall Erskine & Co).

Formation of contract – Offer – Counter-offer – Course of dealings –
Incorporation of standard terms – Exclusion of liability – Unfair Contract Terms Act 1977 – Reasonableness

REES-HOUGH LTD   Plaintiffs

v

REDLAND REINFORCED   Defendants
PLASTICS LTD

Queen's Bench Division   *His Honour Judge*
(Official Referees' Business)   *John Newey QC*
21, 22, 23, 24, 28, 29, 30 November 1983, 1, 5,
6, 7, 8, 12, 13, 14, 15, 19, 20 December 1983,
2 April 1984

Considerations relevant to the reasonableness of an exclusion clause

The plaintiffs, tunnelling contractors, bought pipes from the defendants, manufacturers of pipes, to enable them to perform a contract with
the Thames Water Authority (TWA). The plaintiffs were one of the
leading British specialists in a relatively new form of pipe laying, known
as pipe jacking, which involves the introduction of whole pipes into
tunnels as they are excavated and driving them along the tunnel with
hydraulic jacks. The plaintiffs bought nearly all their supplies of jacking pipes from the defendants and were in turn one of the defendants'
principal customers. The defendants had since 1967 had terms of sale
which appeared on their brochures, estimates and acceptance of order
forms. The senior officers of the plaintiffs were aware that the
defendants had standard terms of sale though they had never studied
them. When defects had appeared in pipes supplied by the defendants
to the plaintiffs, they had been rectified and the defendants had not
sought to rely on the limitations contained in their standard terms.

In September 1979 the plaintiffs were invited by TWA to tender for
a tunnel and pumping station to be built in Surrey. The plaintiffs sent
an inquiry to the defendants. This inquiry contained a statement of the
internal and external diameter of the pipes; the nature of the joints; the
watertightness and the length of the pipe. In later telephone discussions it was stated that the maximum load imposed on the pipes during

jacking would be 400 tonnes and that the maximum angle of deflection (that is the angle between two pipes when they are being joined together) should be 1½°.

In November 1979 the plaintiffs submitted a tender to TWA and on 14 January 1980 TWA accepted the plantiffs' pipe jacking tender. On 25 January the plaintiffs sent their formal order to the defendants and on 30 January the defendants sent a formal acceptance of order which had their terms of sale on the reverse.

The pipes supplied by the defendants were not able to withstand the pressure exerted on them by the plaintiffs' working methods and many of them cracked. The plaintiffs eventually brought an action for breach of contract.

HELD: (1) The defendants' acceptance of order was not an acceptance but a counter-offer. This counter-offer was accepted by the plaintiffs when they accepted the first delivery of pipes. The contract was therefore on the basis of the defendants' standard terms.

(2) *Semble*, there was such a course of dealing between the parties that the defendants' standard terms would have been incorporated into the contract in any event.

(3) The defendants' standard terms apart, the defendants would have been in breach of their implied obligations as to fitness for purpose and merchantability and of an express term that the pipes could be operated at pressures of up to 400 tonnes and angles of deflection of up to 1½°.

(4) The defendants were also under a duty in tort to exercise reasonable care in the design of the pipes.

(5) The defendants' terms were clear and unequivocal and subject to the provisions of the Unfair Contract Terms Act 1977 would have excluded their liability under (3) and (4) above.

(6) However, the terms did not pass the test of reasonableness under that Act and were therefore ineffective to exclude the defendants' liability.

HIS HONOUR JUDGE JOHN NEWEY QC: In this case the plaintiffs, Rees-Hough Ltd (RH), tunnelling and pipe-jacking contractors, have brought an action against Redland Reinforced Plastics Ltd (Redland), who were at all material times manufacturers of concrete pre-cast jacking pipes.

RH claimed damages from Redland for breach of contract. By their amended statement of claim they put their case in various ways: they allege that there was a contract for the sale of pipes, concluded by telephone on 5 November 1979, but subject to a condition which was satisfied on 14 January 1980; alternatively, that there was a contract concluded at a meeting on 21 January 1980; alternatively, that there was a contract concluded by the despatch of RH's order on 25 January 1980.

Whichever contract be proved RH claim that there were express terms in it that the pipes should meet requirements stated by RH and should also be of merchantable quality, reasonably fit for the purpose and designed and manufactured with proper skill and care. If (contrary to RH's contentions) none of the contracts alleged by them came into existence, but a contract was made between the parties on 30 January 1980, or afterwards, the same terms were to be implied in it.

RH further alleged that before any contract for sale was made they entered into what I will call a collateral contract with Redland, whereby in consideration of RH agreeing to submit or submitting a tender to the Thames Water Authority (TWA) Redland promised, *inter alia*, that they would design and manufacture pipes to meet RH's requirements and that their design would be underwritten by a consulting engineer. RH also contend that Redland owed them a duty in negligence.

Finally, RH contend that after defects had developed in the pipes and many difficulties had been encountered, in return for their agreement to Redland carrying out certain remedial work in a cheaper and simpler manner than that which they favoured, Redland undertook to provide insurance indemnity to cover RH's liability to TWA if the repair should prove inadequate.

Redland by their amended defence assert that the only contract between the parties was made by their formal acceptance of order dated 30 January 1980, which incorporated their standard terms of sale, excluding both implied terms and any duty in negligence. They deny any earlier contract, but say that there had been negotiations between the parties. If (contrary to Redland's contentions) there was such a contract, they allege that their standard terms were necessarily implied in it, because of a long course of dealing between the parties. They deny that they undertook to provide an insurance indemnity. They counterclaim for sums alleged to be due to them.

RH by their reply alleged, *inter alia*, that, if Redland's standard terms were incorporated into a contract between them, then they were unreasonable and so contrary to the Unfair Contract Terms Act 1977. I am dealing only with liability in respect of RH's claim. To assist me the parties have agreed questions for the court, which reflect the pleadings and which I will answer one by one after describing what appear to have been the relevant events.

Pipelines can be laid close to ground level by digging trenches, laying in them pipes each of which has a flat and a bell-shaped end, slotting the pipes together with a rubber ring between the flat end of one and the bell end of the next and then filling up the trenches. The weight of the fill may cause settlement beneath the pipes and may push them directly, so that they move out of line one with another. In those circumstances it is very important that the joints between the pipes should maintain continuity, so as to prevent the escape of whatever is in them.

Pipelines can be formed at greater depths by creating them in tunnels, which can be done by hand or mechanically under the protection of tunnelling shields. Pipes formed of segments can be put together beneath the shields, as excavation advances. Fall of earth on to the pipes will be slight and there will be no settlement beneath them, so that they will not move out of line. There will, however, be many joints in the pipes, each a potential source of weakness.

Sometime before 1960 the idea was conceived, originally in Sweden, of introducing into tunnels as they were excavated whole pipes, one behind the other, by driving them along the tunnels with hydraulic jacks. The jacks thrust against a specially constructed concrete thrust wall opposite the mouth of the tunnel in a shaft dug to an appropriate depth. Pressure is applied to a steel thrust ring set against the circumference of the last pipe in the line to be pushed.

Hydraulic power is provided by a power unit at ground level, which is equipped with a gauge to indicate pressure at the unit. In the leads between the unit and the jacks there is some loss of power and, because of friction between the pipes and the ground surrounding them in the tunnels, pressure decreases along the line of pipes in accordance with the distance from the jack. To reduce friction between pipes and ground, lubricants may be introduced into the annulus between the two. To obviate the need for very high pressures on the pipe in the shaft to move the furthest pipes along, specially equipped pipes called "interjacks" are introduced into the line and, when they needed, they can be connected direct to the hydraulic power supply and themselves act as jacks, so that pressure can be applied at one or more places along the line as well as in the shaft.

Compared with formation with segments this new method, known as pipe jacking, involves more equipment but less manpower and is both quicker and cheaper. Once the pipes are laid they are as unlikely to move as ones made from segments and the only joints in them are between pipes. Unfortunately, however careful the pipe jacker, it is quite impossible when pushing pipes end to end to keep them absolutely straight, so that deflections from line are inevitable. Pipes have, therefore, to be capable of withstanding pressure when pushed at angles so that only small areas of them are in contact with each other and also of maintaining continuity. In this they can be assisted by packing made of hardwood or other materials at their ends, which help to form a flexible joint.

Pipe jacking is now widely used in the United States and Japan and to a lesser extent in other parts of the world, including Britain.

RH was founded in 1968 by Mr C. H. Hough and by a Mr Rees, who is no longer with the company. Mr Hough is a Bachelor of Science in Civil Engineering and a Fellow of the Institution of Civil Engineers. He is obviously energetic and able and is universally recognised as being both knowledgeable about and experienced in pipe jacking. He has a pioneering zeal and enthusiasm for the new technology. From its creation RH undertook pipe jacking.

Redland were until 1982 manufacturers of all types of pipe. I am not certain how long they now intend to remain in existence. In 1960 the company by whom Mr Hough was then employed requested Redland to supply them with a pipe for jacking; Redland did so by modifying the type of pipe which they ordinarily sold for laying in trenches by removing the bell end, and it became their standard jacking pipe, available in several diameters, but always with thick walls capable of sustaining considerable pressures, even as point loads.

RH purchased almost all its jacking pipes from Redland; the companies regularly did business together and their officers got to know each other personally. In the year ending 31 March 1979, 7 of the 12 contracts under which Redland supplied jacking pipes were with RH. In the year ending 31 March 1980, 8 out of the 25 jacking pipe contracts were with RH. There were jacking pipe suppliers other than Redland, but not many and the RH equipment was made so as to be used with Redland pipes. Redland maintained a Products Liability Insurance Policy until about 1968, when they cancelled it. In 1966 or 1967 their solicitors drafted terms of sale from them, which from then onwards appeared on their brochures, in estimates and acceptance of order forms. Mr Hough was aware that Redland had terms of sale, although he had never consciously looked at them, but on several occasions when there were defects in pipes Redland compensated RH without mentioning the terms.

In about 1973 RH and five other companies who undertook pipe jacking formed the Pipe Jacking Association (PJA), of which Mr Hough became chairman. The PJA held meetings with the Concrete Pipe Association (CPA), of which Redland were members. A joint technical committee was formed of which Mr Hough was a member and also Mr A. G. Norman, Redland's Technical Director, who has a Bachelor of Science Degree and is a member of the Institution of Civil Engineers.

In February 1975 the PJA produced in conjunction with the CPA *Design and Specification Bulletin 1*, which described pipe jacking and its uses and contained a typical specification. The descriptive part of the bulletin stated that:

"Flexible joints are incorporated in all concrete jacking pipes. The pipes are designed to resist the large forces imposed during installation."

Paragraph (i)6 of the specification stated:

"Tolerances should be agreed in the light of gradient requirements. Unless otherwise ordered, alignment to the finished pipeline should be within a tolerance of plus and minus 75 mm of true line level at any point in the drive. The pipe manufacturer's stated permitted draw or angular deflection must never be exceeded at any individual joint".

Paragraph (ii) stated below (f):

"All concrete pipes for use in pipe jacking shall comply with BS 556 . . . The pipes supplier shall state the permitted draw and maximum angular deflection of each individual joint and these shall not be exceeded at any time during the jacking operation".

at 2:

"All surfaces at the ends of the pipe which transmit load along the axis of the pipe shall: (iii) have an area sufficient to ensure that the pressure under the maximum load applied by the jacks shall not exceed 15 N/mm^2."

and at 3:

"Concrete in the pipe shall have a minimum crushing strength of 65 N/mm^2 when 28 days old".

The gradient referred to in paragraph (i)6 of the specification is the gradient required for flow purposes in the completed pipe. "Permitted draw" refers to the size of gap at a joint between pipes. Mr Hough told me that the PJA and CPA had not been able to agree what should be a normal angle of deflection; the PJA favoured 1½°.

BS 556 allowed pipes to deviate from straightness by 1 mm per 300 mm, so that a pipe 1.83 m long might deviate by 6 mm. If the pipe had an external diameter of 1550 mm, the permitted deflection was 0.22 of a degree. If, when two pipes were joined, the in-built deflections were opposed to each other, the total deflection at a joint might therefore be 0.44 of a degree.

Paragraph 2 stated that the working load in the shaft should not be more than 15 N/mm^2, but, since the crushing strength of the pipe required by paragraph 3 was to be 65 N/mm^2, the end of the pipe should have been capable of taking a load pressure more than four times the stated working load without distress. The same should have applied to pipes at interjacks.

On 28 June 1977, there was a combined meeting of the PJA and CPA attended by Mr Hough and Mr Norman, at which the PJA expressed the view that pipe joint designs could be improved and Mr Hough questioned the need for what the minutes described as "the makers' disclaimer", meaning a statement by the manufacturers of the maximum jacking load to be evenly distributed over the full circumference and area of the pipe end.

On 9 April 1979, there was a meeting of the CPA and PJA; Mr

Hough was present and the minutes record Mr Norman as having also been present, but he is certain that he was not and I think that Mr A. J. Elliott, Redland's Technical Services Manager, attended in his place. However, Mr Norman received a copy of the minutes.

At the meeting the PJA said that they wanted a pipe joint capable of much greater deflection and they mentioned 1.5° for large diameter pipes; the CPA agreed to examine the matter. The PJA also wanted an increase in the end pressure figure of 15 N/mm², which, of course, appeared in the Bulletin specification, and the CPA agreed to examine that also. There was discussion concerning the possibility of a more economic design of jacking pipe.

Mr Hough believed that it would be possible to produce a cheaper pipe by reducing the thickness of walls and by providing instead additional strength by the use of steel bands at joints. He knew that steel bands were so used abroad. I have no doubt that Mr. Hough mentioned his ideas to officers of Redland on many occasions.

Mr Hough was also anxious to speed tunnelling, and an associated company of RH developed a machine to carry out excavation in front of a tunnelling shield. In June 1979 the machine called the Morcon Tunnelling Machine, was demonstrated at RH's premises and among those who saw it in operation on that occasion was Mr Norman.

On 11 September 1979 after discussions extending over 2 years TWA invited RH to tender for a tunnel and pumping station to be built at their Hersham/Esher sewage treatment works. RH were anxious to obtain the contract and Mr Hough believed that they would be successful if they were able to tender in reliance upon using the Morcon and upon pipe jacking with a less expensive pipe.

On 25 September 1979, Mr Hough wrote to Mr G. Smith, Redland's Sales Director, informing him that RH were tendering for a contract in Surrey involving 1 300 m of 1 200 mm tunnel and asking for "a price for [Redland's] cheapest product to do the job". A specification was given, which included: external diameter of pipe 1 550 mm; internal diameter not less than 1 200 mm;" joint "preferably butt type with a band collar of steel or other material for jacking"; watertightness "a mastic or rubber compound to provide a seal with provision for caulking on completion"; and length of pipe 1.83 m. The specification also read "design to be underwritten by a consulting engineer".

When Mr Hough's letter was received by Redland, Mr Norman was on holiday, but Mr Elliott commenced preliminary work, making use of studies which had been carried out earlier in the year in order to provide a company called A. Streeter & Co Ltd with a more economical pipe than Redland's standard pipe.

On Mr Norman's return he learnt of Mr Hough's letter and received a message asking him to telephone Mr Hough. Mr Norman

telephoned on 17 October 1979. He had before him at the time a piece
of paper on which he had written a list of topics for discussion. Partly
during or partly after the conversation Mr Norman made notes of the
discussion on the piece of paper. Both Mr Hough and Mr Norman gave
evidence with regard to the conversation.

I think that during the conversation Mr Hough stressed the need
for Redland to quote a price to him as soon as possible. He and Mr Norman discussed the type of joint which the new pipes might have. Mr
Norman asked what end load, that is to say working load in the shaft,
Mr Hough envisaged. Mr Hough said that RH intended to use two jacks
each with a capacity of 200 tonnes, so that the maximum possible load if
there were to be no loss because of friction would be 400 tonnes. Either
Mr Norman asked what angle of deflection RH required or, more likely,
Mr Hough referred to the angle which the company required. He said
1½°. There was a discussion as to the type of packing material to be
used in the pipe joint. Nothing was said about a consulting engineer
checking the design of the new pipe.

Mr Hough said that in speaking of 1½°, he was referring to the
angle of deflection during jacking and I am sure that he was. Mr Norman said that he was thinking of angle of deflection when the pipeline
came finally to rest. He said that it was a trade term used in connection
with pipes laid in trenches and that on no account would he have agreed
to provide pipes capable of 1½° deflection when under pressure.

I found Mr Norman's evidence in this respect very surprising. He
knew that what RH wanted were pipes which were not to be laid in trenches, but to be jacked in tunnels. If he thought about the matter at all he
must have realised that there was little risk of pipes moving once they
had reached their final resting places, but that the angle through which
they could be jacked was of very great significance, particularly if the walls
of the new pipes were to be substantially thinner than those of Redland's
standard pipe. He should have remembered from the minutes of the PJA
and CPA meeting of 9 April 1979, if not from other sources of information,
that the PJA wanted a pipe which would jack through 1½°. He should
have remembered that the permitted tolerances in the manufacture of
pipes could by themselves result in nearly half a degree of deflection.

I found Mr Norman's evidence as to the 1½° so surprising that I
have considered long and seriously whether it could possibly be true.
However, it is consistent with Mr Norman's subsequent conduct. If he
had had in mind that the pipes were to be capable of being jacked
through 1½° he would surely have instructed Mr Elliot to that effect
and would have checked whether or not they had been designed so as to
do so; yet he did neither of these things. I accept Mr Norman's evidence, but at the same time I conclude that he displayed astonishing
incompetence for a person occupying his position. No doubt Mr Hough

believed that Mr Norman was referring to angle of deflection during jacking as he was.

After the telephone conversation Mr Norman drew on the bottom of the paper on which he had made his notes a possible design for the joints of the new pipe. He passed it to Mr Elliott, who added a further sketch and some rough calculations.

Mr Elliott set to work to design the pipe. Its outer diameter was to be 1 550 mm and its inner 1 350 mm, so that its wall would be 100 mm. Mr Elliott's drawing of 18 October 1979, showed the configuration of its joint, which included a nib and spigot. In the centre of the joint was to be hardboard "or similar approved packing", on the outer side "approved mastic sealant (not supplied by Redland)", on the inner side, space for caulking once the whole pipe was made, and around the joint was to be a mild steel collar, bonded to it by epoxy mortar. The drawing bore the so-called disclaimer disliked by the PJA which read:

"Note: Maximum end thrust not to exceed 400 tonnes uniformly distributed around the end profile of the packing".

After Mr Elliott had completed his initial design, Redland's costs department worked out the cost of producing the new pipe and provided Mr Smith with the figures. He on 5 November telephoned Mr Hough and quoted a price of £109 for the pipe, which Mr Hough regarded as reasonable. RH as long-established customers would have received discounts. Mr Hough said that Redland had always quoted prices to him orally and once quoted they had never sought to alter them. Nothing was said during the conversation about special pipes: either those required for interjack stations or the leading pipe to fit into the Morcon under the shield.

On 8 November RH submitted two tenders to TWA, one based upon construction with segments and the other, much more competitive, based upon pipe jacking. TWA asked Mr Hough to confirm that the pressure on the end surface of a pipe during jacking would not exceed 15 N/mm^2. This corresponded with 350 tonnes and, after making calculations based on the crushing strength of the concrete, Mr Hough was able to provide the neccessary confirmation.

TWA asked for tests to confirm the strength of the new pipe and on 18 December carrried out a test on a smaller pipe from which lessons could be learnt. On 14 January 1980, TWA accepted RH's pipe jacking tender. There was a further test on 21 January, followed by a discussion between Mr Hough and another representative of RH and Mr Norman, Mr Elliott and Mr Smith.

On 25 January Mr Hough wrote to Mr Smith confirming matters which had been agreed on 21 January. They included detail not affecting the basic design of the pipe, that tests on packing of full joint loading would be carried out and when delivery would be effected. On the same day RH sent their formal order to Redland, which included an order for special pipes.

On 30 January Redland sent to RH their formal acceptance of order, which on its front had in small type near the bottom "The above Order is accepted subject to all our Terms of Sale shown overleaf". On the back were the terms of sale expressed so as, *inter alia*, to exclude all other terms and to limit drastically Redland's liability for defects in goods supplied. I will later set out the relevant terms in full. There are a small number of pipe manufacturers and all or most of them have standard terms.

Three tests of pipes and packing were carried out by Redland using early specimens of the new pipe, cut into halves for the purpose. They were each satisfactory: in the third test held on 2 May, crushing of the concrete did not occur until 1 260 tonnes were reached, but none of the tests included tests of pipes when deflected. Mr Hough says that he was present at the first two tests, but not the third which was on 2 May. Mr Norman, Mr Elliott and Mr Smith said that Mr Hough was present at the third test and that after it, during refreshments, he said that, since the tests had been successful, there was no need for the design to be checked by a consulting engineer.

In a report of events prepared by Mr Elliott before leaving Redland's employment in December 1980, he did not record Mr Hough as being present at the third test. There were refreshments after each test, so that does not help to fix the occasion and makes it easier to confuse them. I am inclined to think that Mr Hough did miss the third test, but that after one of the tests something was said about a consulting engineer. I think it clear that RH must have realised that Redland had not specifically sought advice from a consulting engineer concerning the new pipe and yet they made no complaint on that account.

All Redland's drawings of the new pipe bore the so-called disclaimer except for the last to be issued, when at RH's request, it was omitted. RH did not want TWA to be troubled about pressure reading, particularly as TWA had required no more than 350 tonnes when the disclaimer referred to 400 tonnes.

In March RH started work on the basis of a double shift 7 day week. Mr Hough was personally responsible for the pipes and was frequently on site. Mr R. A. Turner, a quantity surveyor and director, was otherwise in overall charge. Mr V. M. Mohlar, an engineer with experience of tunnelling, pipe jacking and use of the Morcon machine, was site agent. RH's foreman and other staff were all experienced in pipe jacking.

Shafts were dug and pipes began to arrive on site. In late June and July a tunnel 55 m long was excavated manually and pipe jacked using hardwood packing and Tokstrip sealant between entrance shaft and shaft 1. On 26 August tunnelling with the Morcon and pipe jacking began between shafts 5 and 4, a distance of 145 m.

The Morcon worked well, but a claystone boulder damaged its starhead, which reduced its cutting diameter. There was still, however, sufficient annular gap for a lubricant and one called Bentonite was injected throughout jacking. Later the Morcon's motor developed a leak.

RH used two 200 tonne jacks. Mr Hough, Mr Turner and Mr Mohlar each said that the gauge on RH's power unit was in American short tons. A short ton is of 2 000 lbs compared with 2 204 lbs in a tonne, so that readings taken on the gauge would represent proportionately smaller pressures in tonnes. Mr Hough said that all RH's gauges registered in short tons, because their equipment was American made. He produced a gauge as an exhibit. Mr Mohlar kept records of loads applied in the shaft in tonnes, and, in doing so made deductions from gauge readings for friction, but none for the difference between short tons and tonnes. RH seem to have paid little attention to the difference until it was suggested that they had overloaded.

Mr Norman, Mr Smith and Mr Elliott each said that the gauge was in tonnes and in this they were supported by the evidence of Mr R. Remington and Mr K. D. Ankerson, respectively TWA's senior engineer and resident engineer on works at Hersham/Esher.

The importance of this conflict is as a test of credibility of RH's witnesses and not as to whether RH overloaded. Sadly, there were occasions when, sometimes with the co-operation of Redland, RH concealed information from TWA and there were other occasions when RH deliberately misled TWA or Redland. I have referred already to the deletion of the 400 tonnes maximum thrust note from Mr Elliott's drawing before a copy of it was sent to TWA and I will in due course mention other more serious instances. Mr Turner would seem to have been the major offender.

It would undoubtedly have been much more honourable of RH to have been frank and truthful at all times, but there is nonetheless a difference between what may perhaps be called, somewhat euphemistically, trickiness, and what could only amount to conspiracy between RH's witnesses to commit perjury. Mr Hough and Mr Mohlar were the most concerned with the gauge and they impressed me favourably; I think it unlikely that they agreed together to deceive the court.

The Redland and TWA witnesses looked at the gauge simply in order to read it. They were not to know that how its units were described was to be the subject of subsequent dispute. They probably assumed at the time that the gauge was in tonnes and, as a result, now believe that it was. On balance I conclude that RH's witnesses were right when they said that the gauge was in short tons.

I think that Mr Hough and the RH team made full use of their very considerable expertise and also went about the tunnelling and pipe jacking with as much care as they could. They made continual adjustments to maintain line and level, took measures between pipes in order to check angles and deflection, took special care with packing and generally ensured that the pressures on the ends of the pipes in the shaft were of the order of 350 tonnes and so well within both Redland's and generally within TWA's maxima. I have no doubt that they made certain that the pressure rings were correctly adjusted, so that loads were evenly applied. After 34 pipes an interjack was installed and after 41 pipes it was actuated.

All went well until the afternoon of Friday 26 September when Mr Mohlar noticed a fine longitudinal crack in a pipe. He informed Redland, who said that they would be unable to send anyone to inspect until the following Monday. Mr Mohlar had to bring jacking to a stop. On Monday Mr Harris of Redland and Mr Mohlar inspected all the pipes; cracks were observed in five. Mr Harris told Mr Mohlar that the cracks were surface only and that there was nothing to worry about. Mr Mohlar resumed jacking, having to apply a greater pressure than usual in order to start the line moving again and so exceeding TWA's maximum.

On 30 September cracks appeared in a sixth pipe and soon became progressively worse. Cracks also appeared in other pipes. Between 30 September and 5 October 12 pipes were introduced into the line, making 66 in all, and the end of the tunnel was approaching. On 5 October the joint between two pipes failed and jacking was again stopped. On 6 October on the advice of Mr Harris, RH attempted a repair of the joint. On the resumption of pipe jacking on 7 October the joint failed again and for the first time defects in the concrete were found. At about the same time some movement began to appear in the thrust wall in the shaft.

On 10 October, Mr Hough, who had had to be absent abroad during the preceding week, returned to find work at a standstill. He decided to withdraw the Morcon and to finish the execution of the tunnel manually. He introduced two additional 200 tonnes jacks into the shaft. He used all four jacks pushing against the thrust wall to close the gap between the two pipes whose joint had broken, and to start the line moving. This was in the nature of a calculated risk, the pressure was too great and the last pipe failed.

Pipe jacking from shafts 5 to 4 was therefore abandoned and the pipeline was completed by construction in segments.

Mr Elliott, who had visited the site on 8 October, did so again on 11 October. He blamed the earlier failure of the pipes which he had designed upon incorrect adjustment of the jacking ring and those of 10 October upon excessive pressure; I think that he was wrong as to the former, but clearly right as to the latter. RH, in order to prevent TWA

from losing faith in them and in their methods, erroneously represented to them that they had withdrawn the Morcon so that it could be
repaired and had stopped pipe jacking because of the state of the thrust
wall. In fact Mr Hough had begun, first, to have doubt about hardwood
as a packing and, secondly, to think that there was something fundamentally wrong with the pipes.

On 15 October RH began manual excavation, coupled with pipe
jacking from shaft 3 to shaft 2, which was 160 m. A composite material,
Flexcell, was used in place of hardwood. The pipe jack progressed satisfactorily until 18 November, when the steel band on a pipe which was
still partly in the shaft broke. It and the pipe in front of it were removed,
but the later was found to have a nib which was spalled. Redland were
informed. On 26 November another pipe band broke and on 27 November the lead pipe spalled, apparently because the reinforcement on it
was in the wrong place. On 30 November, when about 50 per cent of the
tunnel had been completed, Mr Mohlar found cracks in many pipes and
jacking was abandoned. RH feared that if TWA learnt of this they
would insist upon removal of all the pipes which had been installed,
and therefore informed them that the stopping of pipe jacking was due
to the state of the thrust wall in shaft 3. This wall was leaning back-
wards because a heading timber behind it had moved, due to the presence of water, but it could have been made good at relatively small cost.

Subsequently the tunnel from shafts 3 to 2 was completed in
segments and all remaining tunnels at Hersham/Esher were either
completed in the same way or by sub-contractors using a pipe jacking
method of their own. RH's contract with TWA had become for them a
disaster in terms of monetary losses and possibly loss of reputation.

During the period when pipe jacking from Shafts 3 to 2 was still
proceeding, Mr Mohlar and Mr Ankerson carried out a detailed examination of the completed line shafts 5 to 4. They found numerous
defects in the pipes, which were set out in a list forwarded by TWA to
RH under cover of a letter of 27 November. In the following January an
investigation of pipes in line shafts 3 to 2 revealed that their condition
was similar.

On 5 January 1981, there was a meeting between Mr Hough and
Mr Turner and Mr Norman and Mr Smith, of which Mr Turner and Mr
Smith each made contemporaneous notes. At the meeting Mr Hough
said that he thought that the third trial test had given a false impression
and that the pipes were not capable of sustaining a load of more than
200 tonnes. He asked whether the pipes had been designed to take $1\frac{1}{2}°$
deflection during jacking and received in reply Mr Norman's expla-
nation of what he had understood by $1\frac{1}{2}°$ deflection. Mr Norman said
that many of the existing cracks would close autogenously. The question was raised whether if TWA demanded a guarantee of the pipes for

30 years Redland would provide one. At the meeting or within the next few days Redland agreed, *inter alia*, to make good spalling in the pipes with epoxy mortar. They, for the first time, mentioned their standard terms.

By letter of 16 January RH put forward what was in substance Redland's offer of repairs to TWA, who, after a meeting, by letter of 29 January, required that there should first be a further investigation. On 26 January Mr Hough suggested that TWA might consider an extended guarantee and TWA indicated that they would do so.

On 13 February Redland instructed Mr A. C. Paterson of Bullen & Partners, consultant engineers, to inspect line 5 to 4 and to report to them. He submitted an interim report on 20 February, which described faults in the pipes, made some adverse comments as to line and level and suggested remedial action. On 24 February Mr Hough and Mr Smith met, when it was agreed that a copy of Mr Paterson's report, from which the comments had been excised, should be sent to TWA. Mr Smith offered RH £58 000 as compensation, which was rejected as totally inadequate. The edited interim report was sent on 25 February. Mr Paterson later submitted a further report, which was substantially in the same terms as the interim.

On 9 March RH, after correspondence with TWA and Redland, called upon Sir William Halcrow & Partners to produce a report advising as to remedial measures. In April Halcrows submitted a report, which among other things recommended more elaborate remedial measures than had Mr Paterson. RH sent copies of the report to TWA and to Redland; the latter did not agree that Halcrow's more extensive and expensive measures were necessary.

On 2 June Mr A. D. Kindred, RH's contracts director, reached agreement with TWA for the lesser remedial measures advised by Mr Paterson, but soon afterwards RH received a letter from Halcrow's urging the necessity for those which they had recommended. On 11 June Mr Turner wrote to Redland asking them to reconsider the matter and saying:

> "If you still consider the currently agreed measures are adequate, we shall require some form of assurance from you to protect us on our latent defects liability".

About 22 June there was a telephone conversation between Mr Norman and Mr Kindred. Mr Norman said that Redland were ready to proceed with the repairs. Mr Kindred said that RH would not agree to them doing so, unless provided with the assurance for which they had asked. Mr Norman said that Mr Kindred used the words "insurance assurance". I think that the conversation ended with Mr Norman undertaking to take the matter up with his superior, a Mr Marriage, and to telephone back. Mr Kindred stated that about two days later, not having heard from Mr Norman, he telephoned him, and Mr Norman said that he had been authorised to provide RH with an insurance indemnity. Mr Norman told me that he had spoken to Mr Marriage and that a second telephone conversation with Mr Kindred took place, but that he did not say that he had been authorised to provide an insurance indemnity. Mr Norman said that what he said to Mr Kindred was that neither he nor Mr Marriage understood what was required.

On 29 June Mr Turner wrote to Redland for the "Attention of Mr A. G. Norman" a letter in which he wrote:

"We confirm that you have notified our Mr Kindred that you consider the remedial measures adequate and that you will be providing us with insurance indemnity to cover our latent defects liability."

The letter could easily have been self-serving and another one of RH's tricks. Mr Norman said that it was quite untrue, but, strangely if that be so, when he replied on 9 July he wrote merely:

"Regarding your reference to insurance, we have passed this to our Company Solicitor for further attention".

Mr Kindred was undoubtedly a more impressive witness than Mr Norman and, in view of the letters and since it is very hard to believe that senior officials of a large company did not understand what was meant by an insurance indemnity, I accept Mr Kindred's account of the second telephone conversation rather than Mr Norman's.

In a letter of 10 July, signed on behalf of Mr Mohlar, RH wrote to Redland:

"We await outstanding details of . . . insurance indemnity before we can give final approval and acceptance of your work".

Mr Norman replied on 23 July 1981:

"Regarding the insurance indemnity with remedial work, this is being dealt with by the appropriate Department within the Group".

On 22 July Mr Turner telephoned Mr Norman, who circulated a memorandum describing the conversation on the same date. One item in it recorded that RH required the insurance indemnity requested for Redland's remedial work as soon as possible.

In the meanwhile both Redland and RH carried out most of the works which had been agreed with TWA. On 24 July Mr Turner wrote stating untruthfully that TWA would not approve of works until Redland provided the indemnity policy. On 4 August Mr Norman suggested that RH submitted a draft of what they envisaged. Mr Turner told me that on receipt of the letter he telephoned Mr Norman and suggested a simple policy "with the Pru", but Mr Norman said that he did not remember the telephone call.

On 5 August Mr Norman who had consulted Redland's solicitors wrote a letter on Redland's behalf warranting that their treatment of the pipes complied with the specification for the supply of pipes by them to RH.

Mr Turner telephoned on 10 August and, according to a memorandum of Mr Norman, said that the warranty did not meet RH's requirements, as their liability to TWA would continue for 10 years, but that he was not concerned whether Redland had insurance to cover such an event. Mr Norman wrote in reply to the telephone call, saying that Redland could not go further until they knew what claims RH were bringing.

On 28 August Mr Turner wrote another letter stating untruthfully that:

"The current situation is that TWA will not accept the repaired line 5 to 4 without an indemnification from ourselves".

By "ourselves" Mr Turner presumably meant "yourselves". The letter went on to say that Mr Norman had promised an "acceptable document".

After a meeting between Mr Hough on 9 September and a letter from RH of 17 September asking for an indemnity linked to an insurance policy, Redland proffered an indemnity for the length of RH's liability. This was in itself satisfactory for RH, provided that Redland does not go into liquidation. On 21 October Redland's solicitors denied that RH were entitled to any insurance cover, but by then RH had put forward a claim for damages in excess of three quarters of a million pounds.

To conclude this description of the facts, after considering the reports and evidence of Mr Kirkland of Halcrow's and Mr Taylor of Bullen & Partners, I am left with the conviction that at the very least what was wrong with Redland's pipes was that they could not have sustained pressure of 400 tonnes even through an angle of deflection of 0.44° which their own tolerance in manufacture permitted, and that they were certainly not designed to take any greater angle. Since it is impossible to pipe jack in a completely straight line, the pipes were unfit to be jacking pipes.

The first question to the court is:

When was a contract for the sale of pipe jacking pipes concluded?
Was it
(a) On 5 November 1979 (as a conditional contract, which condition was satisfied on 14 January 1980); or
(b) On 21 January 1980 (at the meeting at Graylands); or
(c) On 25 January 1980 (when RH sent/posted their order); or were facts on (a), (b) and (c) matters of preliminary negotiations only?; or
(d) On 30 January 1980 (when Redland sent the acceptance of order); or
(e) On a later date when RH accepted and paid for pipes supplied by Redland (ie if (d) were deemed a counter-offer by reason of the terms and conditions?).

I think that Mr Hough's letter of 25 September 1979, the telephone conversation between Mr Hough and Mr Norman on 17 October, the telephone convesation between Mr Hough and Mr Smith on 5 November, and the discussion between Mr Hough, an employee of RH, Mr Norman, Mr Elliott and Mr Smith on 21 January 1980, constituted enquiry, refining of requirements, and negotiations between RH and Redland. None of them resulted in a concluded contract for the sale of jacking pipes, although they could give rise to terms which became incorporated in a contract.

I think that RH's order of 25 January, which gave particulars of the number of types of pipes required and of delivery and also referred to price "as agreed", was an offer to enter into a contract. Redland's "acceptance of order" of 30 January set out the price which had been agreed for ordinary pipes on 5 November, but gave different prices for special pipes and in addition made their purported acceptance subject to their conditions of sale. I think that Redland's document did not, despite its description, constitute an acceptance of RH's offer, but a counter-offer, which RH were free to accept or to reject as they thought fit.

RH did not reply either orally or in writing to Redland, but in due course and after the crushing tests had been concluded, they began to take delivery of Redland's pipes. I think that it was on receipt of the first pipes that RH accepted Redland's counter offer and a contract of sale came into existence. The conclusion of the contract was not postponed until RH made their first payment for pipes.

I will take questions 2, 6 and 7 together; in answering them I will not take into account the possible effect of Redland's standard terms. The questions are:

2 *Was it an express term of any such contract as is found, that Redland's pipes should be capable of being jacked at 400 tonnes evenly distributed around the full profile of the pipe, in the shaft or at the inter-jack and with angles of up to 1½° deflection between pipes in the drive? Or was it for RH to make empirical allowace for angles of deflection should they occur?*

6 *Are there implied conditions of the contract of sale as found:*
(i)   *As to merchantable quality;*
(ii) *As to reasonable fitness for purpose:*
(iii) *Skill and care in the design and manufacture of the pipes?*

7 *Was it part of the implied condition as to reasonable fitness for purpose of the contract of sale as found that the pipes should be capable of being jacked at 400 tonnes uniformly distributed around the full profile of the packing in the pit or at the inter-jack and with angular deflections in the pipeline*
(i)   *1½° [to 2° or slightly more]; or*
(ii) *A practical angle;*
or was it for the contractor to manage his pipeline to take account of the degrees of deflection occurring?

The contract between Redland and RH was for the sale of goods, namely, pipes for jacking. An essential characteristic of such pipes, which makes them different from all other types of pipe, is that they must be capable of sustaining high pressures when at angles one to another. There is obviously an important continuing relationship between load and angle.

Neither RH's order of 25 January nor Redland's so-called acceptance of order referred to maximum end thrusts or to angles of deflection between pipes, but they had been mentioned during the telephone conversation between Mr Hough and Mr Norman on 17 October.

On that occasion Mr Hough told Mr Norman clearly what RH wanted, namely, a pipe which could be jacked at 400 tonnes in the shaft with pipes in the line at angles of $1\frac{1}{2}°$. Mr Norman did not say expressly that Redland would provide what was required, but he raised no objection and they went on to discuss other requirements. In fact Mr Norman had misunderstood what Mr Hough meant by angle of deflection, but, for the reasons which I have given previously, he should not have done so. Mr Hough had no reason to believe that they were not *ad idem* and that Mr Norman had not agreed to what RH wanted.

Nothing was written or said subsequently by Redland to indicate that they were not providing pipes to meet RH's requirements or that they were expecting RH to avoid overstressing the pipes by making empirical allowances for angles of deflection.

Because of the telephone conversation I think that when a contract was concluded between RH and Redland, it was an express term of it that the jacks should be capable of being jacked at 400 tonnes evenly distributed around the profile of the pipe when in the shaft, or at an inter-jack, with angles of up to $1\frac{1}{2}°$ between pipes in the line.

If I am wrong in deciding that there was an express term, it becomes material to consider whether there were implied terms. Redland sold jacking pipes in the course of their business, Redland did not bring to RH's attention their limitation in jacking and RH could not on examining the pipes have discovered it, therefore, under s 14(2) of the Sale of Goods Act 1979, there was an implied term that the pipes should be of merchantable quality.

Again Redland sold the pipes in the course of their business and RH expressly brought to their notice by the letter of the 25 September and subsequently that they were required for jacking, therefore, under s 14(3) of the 1979 Act, there was an implied condition that the pipes would be reasonably fit for jacking.

It may be that there was room for a further implied term requiring Redland to have exercised skill and care in the design of the pipes and that performance of that term demanded that they should have taken into account deflection during jacking, but in my view such a term would have added nothing to those implied under the Sale of Goods Act, and there was no need to infer one.

In 1979 the PJA were pressing for a pipe joint capable of $1\frac{1}{2}°$ under pressure and the CPA were examining the proposal. The new pipe to be made by Redland for sale to RH followed earlier discussions between representatives of the companies and was intended to be a technological advance.

Against this background I think that for the pipes to have been of merchantable quality and/or fit for purpose they should have been capable of being jacked at 400 tonnes uniformly distributed in the shaft or inter-jack at angles of $1\frac{1}{2}°$ or at any rate approaching $1\frac{1}{2}°$. I think that if the pipes had been capable of taking say $1\frac{1}{4}°$ that would have sufficed. They could not have been expected to sustain $2°$.

Question 2A is:

Was it an express term of any such contract as is found, that Redland's design should be underwritten by a consulting engineer?

That the design should be underwritten was one of the requirements of Mr Hough's specification letter of 25 September, but it was never mentioned again, except either in passing or dismissively after one of the tests held after Redland's acceptance of order. I do not think that it ever became a term of the contract.

Question 3 is:

Was there a collateral contract as alleged in paragraph 20 of the statement of claim, or were these facts preliminary negotiations only, or was there any consideration?

I think that this turns on the effect of the telephone conversation between Mr Hough and Mr Smith on 5 November; when Mr Smith quoted to Mr Hough a price for the proposed new pipe, so as to enable RH to submit a tender to TWA.

Prices had been quoted in similar conversations on previous occasions and Redland had never sought to change them. Unless, of course, RH could rely on Redland adhering to their quotations for a reasonable time RH could not safely submit a tender to anyone else. Unless RH submitted tenders, they would not obtain contracts and, therefore, not buy pipes from Redland.

It was for the companies' mutual benefit that Redland did not change a quotation once given, but it does not follow that there was contractual obstacle in the way of Redland doing so. It depends *inter alia* on what the parties intended.

As the result of Redland quoting a price, RH did not become obliged to submit a tender and, if they did so, they were not prevented from withdrawing it. If they had obtained a better quotation from someone other than Redland, they could have tendered on the basis of it rather than Redland's. When the conversation occurred on 5

November, there was still much to be investigated and decided upon in connection with the proposed new pipe.

In my opinion the telephone conversation was, as I have said previously, part of the negotiations, which led eventually to a concluded contract. It did not create a contract by itself, because neither RH nor Redland intended that it should give rise to legal relations between them. There was no collateral contract.

Question 4 is:

If the contract of sale is found to be as per 1(a), (b) or (c) were Redland's standard terms and conditions of sale incorporated by implication from the prior course of dealings between the parties and from RH's knowledge of them?

I have already held that the contract for sale was not as put in questions 1(a), (b) or (c), but for the purpose of answering this question I will assume that I am wrong.

Redland adopted standard terms of sale one or two years before RH were incorporated and became their customers. The terms appeared on all copies of Redland's trading literature. Mr Hough knew throughout that Redland had standard terms, although he had never studied them. It may be inferred from the previous dealings that other officers and employees of RH knew of the terms' existence.

I think that Redland's terms of sale would have been implied in any contract made in accordance with 1(a) or 1(b) or 1(c).

Question 5 is:

If the contract of sale is as per 1(d) or (e) are the standard terms expressly incorporated?

I have held that in substance the contract was as per 1(e), so that the standard terms were referred to on the face and set out on the back of a contractual document. They, therefore, clearly became express terms of the contract. I would have reached the same conclusion had I thought that the contract had been as per 1(d).

Question 8 is:

Is there a tortious duty of care in addition to the contractual duty; and if so, were Redland negligent as alleged in paragraphs 28(3) and (7) of the amended statement of claim?

The sub-paragraphs allege failure to design with proper care and skill, failure to warn RH before they became contractually bound or afterwards that they had been unable to design for 1½° deflection and/or that they had not obtained underwriting by a consulting engineer.

The proximity between Redland and RH was such that Redland must have foreseen that if they did not exercise reasonable care in relation to the pipes RH were likely to suffer damage. I think, therefore, that Redland owed to RH a duty of care in negligence.

Fulfilment of this duty no doubt required Redland to exercise reasonable care in the design of pipes which Redland were going to supply to RH for jacking. This was I think the essence of Redland's duty in negligence. To allege, as does the amended statement of claim, that there was a duty to warn that the pipes had not been designed to take 1½° is I think an over-elaboration. I do not think that there was any duty in tort to warn that a consulting engineer had not underwritten the design. Redland's duty in negligence merely repeated contractual obligations.

Question 9 is:

In any event do Redland's standard terms and conditions on their proper construction (numbers 1 and 10 in particular) exclude liability for such breach of any of the above terms as may be found? If so are those terms and conditions fair and reasonable between the parties in the light of the circumstances which were, or ought reasonably to have been, in the contemplation of the parties at the date of the contract?

The relevant terms of sale are 1 and 10, which read:

"(1) *Application of Terms*

All sales of goods made by the Company shall be on these terms. In the event of any person (. . . "the customer") giving an order to the Company which is purported to be accepted by the Company, a contract shall be concluded between the customer and the Company . . . to which these terms shall apply to the exclusion of any other terms, warranties or representations, written or oral, express or implied, even if contained in the customer's order,"

and term 10:

"*Quality and Description*

The Company warrants that the goods shall be of sound workmanship and materials and in the event of a defect in any goods being notified to the Company in writing immediately upon the discovery thereof which is the result of unsound workmanship or materials, the Company will, at its own cost at its option, either repair or replace the same, provided always that the Company shall be liable only in respect of defects notified within three months of delivery of the goods concerned. Save as aforesaid the Company undertakes no liability, contractual or tortious, in respect of loss or damage suffered by the customer as a result of any defect in the goods (even if attributable to unsound workmanship or materials) or as a result of any warranty, representation, conduct or negligence of the Company, its directors, employees or Agents, and all terms of any nature, express or implied, statutory or othewise, as to correspondence with any particular description or sample, fitness for purpose or merchantability are hereby excluded".

These terms are I think clear and unequivocal and, subject to the question of whether they are reasonable under the Unfair Contract Terms Act 1977, they have the effect of excluding the express and implied terms to which I have referred when answering questions 2, 6 and 7.

They also have the effect of excluding liability in negligence. See as to the exclusion of negligence by contract Lord Roskill in *Junior Books* v *Veitchi Ltd* [1983] AC 520 at p 546 and the Court of Appeal in *William Hill* v *Bernard Sunley* (1982) 22 BLR 1 at p 26 and, perhaps I may add, my own decision in *H. W. Nevill (Sunblest) Ltd* v *William Press & Son Ltd* (1980) 20 BLR 78 at p 92.

The Unfair Contract Terms Act 1977, section 3 reads (omitting irrelevant words):

"(1) This section applies as between contracting parties where one of them deals . . . on the other's written standard terms of business.

(2) As against that party, the other cannot by reference to any contract term –

(a) When himself in breach of contract, exclude or restrict any liability of his in respect of the breach . . .

except insofar as . . . the contract term satisfies the requirements of reasonableness".

S 6(3) of the Act provides that liability for breach of obligations under what is now s 14 of the Sale of Goods Act 1979 (merchantable quality and fitness for purpose) "can be excluded or restricted by reference to a contract term, but only insofar as the term satisfies the requirement of reasonableness".

Under s 11(1) "the requirement of reasonableness . . . is that the term shall have been a fair and reasonable one to be included having regard to the circumstances which were, or ought reasonably to have been, known to or in the contemplation of the parties when the contract was made".

S 11(2) provides that "In determining for the purposes of s 6 . . . whether a contract term satisfies the requirement of reasonableness, regard should be had in particular to the matters specified in Schedule 2 to the Act". These can be summarised as follows:

(a) strength of the bargaining positions;

(b) whether the customer received an inducement to agree to the term, or had an opportunity of entering into a similar contract with others, without such a term;

(c) whether the customer knew of the term;

(d) where the contract excludes or restricts liability for breach of condition, whether it was reasonable to expect compliance with it; and

(e) whether the goods were manufactured to the special order of the customer.

S 11(5) provides that "It is for those claiming that a contract term . . . satisfies the requirement of reasonableness to show that it does".

S 3 would appear capable of saving both express and implied

terms, whereas s 6(3) is only concerned with those implied by s 14 of the Sale of Goods Act. There is no requirement that Schedule 2 matters should be taken into account in deciding "reasonableness" for the purposes of s 3, but it seems sensible to do so.

In *George Mitchell (Chesterhall) Ltd* v *Finney Lock Seeds Ltd* [1983] 3 WLR 163 the House of Lords considered the requirement of reasonableness in the context of the modified s 55 of the Sale of Goods Act 1979, as set out in paragraph 11 of Schedule I to the Act, replacing the law as contained in the Supply of Goods (Implied Terms) Act 1973, which differed from the 1977 Act in that circumstances at the date of the defendants' breach of contract could be taken into account and the onus of proving unreasonableness was upon the plaintiff.

The plaintiff in *Mitchell* v *Finney* had purchased what purported to be special winter cabbage seed from the defendants, but it proved to be inferior autumn cabbage seed. The price paid for the seed was small and the damages claimed very large. The defendants attempted to rely upon conditions endorsed upon their invoice, which limited their liability to replacing the seeds or refunding the price and excluded all conditions and warranties. The House of Lords, upholding the courts below, held that the defendants' conditions were unreasonable.

Lord Bridge of Harwich, with whose speech other members of the House agreed, said at p 171 that in deciding what is reasonable:

". . . the court must entertain a whole range of considerations, put them in the scales of one side or the other, and decide at the end of the day on which side the balance comes down".

Lord Bridge at p 172 identified as relevant considerations whether the defendants knew of the conditions, would have had any difficulty as laymen in understanding them, relative bargaining strength, whether similar limitation of liability was universally embodied in terms of trade between seedsmen and farmers, whether the limitation had been negotiated between representative bodies and, most important, whether it had been the defendants' practice to negotiate settlements of claims for damages in excess of the price of the seeds, so showing whether they thought the conditions fair.

In the present case RH can, I think, be regarded as having contracted on standard terms and the contract was for the sale of goods. Considerations which in my view support Redland's contention that their standard conditions are reasonable are: that the contract was between two companies and, while Redland were the larger, RH were capable of looking after themselves; all or most other concrete pipe manufacturers contract on the basis of standard terms; the PJA did not protest at such terms, although they had with regard to statements of limitations on loading; RH had long been aware that Redland had standard terms; the terms would have been understandable by any intelligent businessman; and RH never attempted to negotiate alterations in the terms.

Considerations urged on behalf of Redland as proving reasonableness which I do not accept are: Mr Hough's expertise – I think that
his skills were in jacking rather than in design and that he relied upon
Redland; the pipes were being designed in a hurry – I think that
Redland had adequate time in which to design the pipes properly themselves or, if necessary, to bring in a consultant such as Bullen to do so,
but, if they felt that they were short of time, they should have said so;
and Redland would have had no control over what happened on site –
true, but irrelevant, since if misuse of the pipes caused damage,
Redland would not be liable.

Considerations which in my opinion are against Redland's contention that the terms are reasonable are that: RH were regular customers
of Redland and major purchasers of their jacking pipes; when in the
past pipes had been defective, Redland had not relied on the terms, but
had paid compensation to RH; Redland did not refer to the terms during negotiation of the contract; the sums to be paid by RH for the pipes
were substantial; Redland was likely to gain from the development of a
new pipe, which after successful use could be marketed generally; the
remedies of repair and replacement provided by the terms were inapt if
defects were liable to result in pipe jacking having to be abandoned
when a pipeline was incomplete; the terms had not been negotiated
between the PJA and the CPA or any other trade associations; and
Redland could, as it had before 1968, have maintained product liability
insurance.

A consideration put forward by RH which I do not accept is that
the defects in the pipes were caused by Redland's lack of care; that is
something which I could only take into account if allowed to consider
the position when the breaches of contract occurred.

Turning to the schedule 2 guidelines; as to (a) and (c), I have
already referred to the parties' bargaining position and to RH's knowledge of the terms; (b), RH did not receive an inducement to agree to
the terms – they received a normal trade discount – there was no evidence as to whether they could have purchased pipes from another
supplier without the terms but at a higher price; (d), at the time of the
contract Redland, as experienced pipe manufacturers could have been
expected to produce satisfactory pipes; and (e), the pipes were ordered
by RH, but they did not prescribe the design, which the guideline seems
to require.

Obviously some considerations carry much more weight than
others; for example that RH did not lack the ability to look after themselves is probably the weightiest in favour of upholding the terms; and,
for example, that Redland have never in the past sought to rely upon
the terms in its dealings with RH may well be the weightiest against.

Doing the best I can, I reach the conclusion that Redland have failed to prove that their standard terms were reasonable; indeed I think that the balance of the considerations is strongly against the terms being reasonable.

I therefore hold that Redland cannot rely upon the standard terms of sale to invalidate the express and implied terms between themselves and RH.

Questions 10 and 11 I will take together. They are:

Did pipe-jacking in pipelines 5–4 and 3–2 have to be abandoned? If so, was it in each case because of breach of contract and/or negligence or was it because of RH's site practice in relation to alignment and thrusting loads, steering, thrust walls, thrusting ring and/or packing?

I think that on lines 5–4 and on 3–2 pipe jacking had to be abandoned and that the reason for abandonment of each line was the failure of the pipes, due to their inability to be jacked at pressures in the shaft and at interjacks, which were below 400 tonnes. I think, therefore, that each abandonment was caused by Redland's breaches of contract and/or negligence.

I do not think that RH's site practice was in any way responsible for either abandoment. Undoubtedly, RH caused the total failure of the last pipe in line 5–4 by overloading, but by that time other pipes had failed and abandonment was inevitable. I think that through no fault of RH at the dates of abandonment the thrust walls serving both lines needed attention. Since the end of line 5–4 had almost been reached, RH might have been able to finish jacking that line without carrying out substantial repairs to the wall. On line 3–2 I am sure that major repairs would have been required. The repairs would have taken days rather than weeks, after which pipe jacking could have been resumed.

Question 12 is:

Did Redland agree to provide insurance indemnity in or about June 1981? If so, was there consideration for such agreement? If so, is the agreement sufficiently certain? Is such agreement if found, enforceable by specific performance?

The question of Redland providing RH with "some form of assurance" was first raised with Redland by Mr Turner's letter dated 11 June. Before that Mr Kindred had put Redland's proposals to TWA thereby indicating RH's consent to Redland carrying them out, and had obtained TWA's approval of them. The letter of 11 June quite rightly asks Redland to reconsider, for the matter had already been decided; RH could not properly retract the consent, which they had given. If Redland ever gave an undertaking to provide RH with an assurance or insurance indemnity, there would, I think, have been no consideration for their undertaking.

I have endeavoured to summarise previously the tangled history of the communications between RH and Redland. I am by no means sure that Redland ever promised anything, but, if they did, it was by no means clear what it was. If there had been consideration to support a simple agreement, its terms would have been insufficiently clear for it to have had legal validity.

If there had been a valid agreement, I doubt whether it would have been enforceable by specific performance, as I would have thought that damages sufficient to enable RH to arrange insurance for themselves would have been an adequate remedy.

The last question is:

If Redland are not in breach of contract, are RH in breach of the contract of sale by cancelling their pipe order?

For reasons which I have already given I think that Redland were in breach of contract, so that RH were entitled to cancel their order for pipes not already delivered.

During the course of this judgment I have said little about the experts, but in fact they were both of considerable assistance to me in seeking to understand the technologies and problems involved.

Finally, I should like to express my gratitude to Mr Garland who appeared for Redland and to Mr Dyson who appeared for RH and to their respective juniors and solicitors for the outstanding efficient way in which this case was prepared and presented, which undoubtedly resulted in considerable saving of both time and costs without loss in other respects.

COUNSEL

For the plaintiffs: Mr John Dyson QC and Mr Vivian Ramsey (instructed by Messrs Alan Wilson & Co).

For the defendants: Mr Patrick Garland QC and Mr Richard Gray (instructed by Messrs McKenna & Co).

Index of Cases

Index of Statutes and Statutory Instruments

Including Rules of the Supreme Court

Building Contract Dictionary

Vincent Powell-Smith and David Chappell

The *Building Contract Dictionary* is the ultimate reference book for all those concerned with contract administration, from architects and quantity surveyors to contractors and solicitors. It provides authoritative answers to these and many other questions which are troublesome in practice. Its clarity of style and lack of pomposity will also make it immediately welcome to the layman—to clients who want to know what their solicitors are talking about—and to students in the building industry. It defines and explains in detail not only those words and phrases which might cause difficulty in connection with building contracts, but also the concepts encountered in relation to contracts, such as 'standard of care' or 'foreseeability'.

Within the definitions, the *Dictionary* also refers constantly to relevant legal cases; these cases not only illustrate more clearly the definitions in question, but they also provide suitable quotes from the judgments themselves

234 × 148 mm   approx 480 pp   ISBN 0–85139–758–1   cloth

AJ Legal Handbook
Fourth edition

Edited by Anthony Speaight and Gregory Stone

Law affects the practice of architecture in more and more ways, and to an increasing degree. This book has become a standard text for students and an essential office reference for architects and related professionals in the building industry.

The contents of the fourth edition reflect the various new developments in case law, particularly land law, the law of negligence and the law of limitations. Forms of contract such as the JCT form have been amended, and professional codes of practice have been revised.

Contents

Introduction to English law
Introduction to Scots law
English land law
Scottish land Law
Building contracts
Building contracts in Scotland
The liability of architects
Arbitration
Statutory authorities in England and Wales
Statutory authorities in Scotland

Planning law
English construction regulations
Construction regulations in Scotland
Copyright
Architects and the law of employment
Legal organisation of architects' offices
Architect's appointment
Professional conduct in England
Professional conduct in Scotland

'This is undoubtedly a comprehensive and authoritative guide to those areas of law of particular concern to architects and other professions involved in the building industry.'

Local Government Chronicle

297 × 210 mm   *254 pp*   *ISBN 0–85139–751–4*   *paper*

The Architect's Guide to Fee Negotiations

Ray Moxley

Competitive fee tendering is now a reality of architectural practice. Closely following the RIBA *Plan of Work*, this new book sets all the items that have to be negotiated at each stage, so that costs can be assigned to them and the work of all the members of the building team noted and priced. It thus serves as a check list, a negotiating instrument and a financial working tool.

Contents
The full form
The short form
Conditions of appointment
Recommended fees and expenses
Appendix: Costing work in the professional office
Software manual for Feemaster

'Should earn the gratitude of all architects in private practice who wish to survive in a competitive world.'

John Partridge, Chairman, ACA

210 × 297 mm   160 pp   ISBN 0–946228–05–1   paper

Professional Liability

Ray Cecil

Architects are now more than ever vulnerable to legal actions, which may occur long after a building has been completed, and due to inflation may involve far larger sums than the cost of the original building. The law here is complex; how to practise safely while still providing a professional service has become a major concern of the whole profession.

Ray Cecil is an architect writing for architects, to 'advise, guide and horribly warn' them. The reader is taken through various situations and is shown what the law seemed to be, and what actually happened. The author deals in depth with the problems of suitable and adequate insurance. He offers a combination of experienced professional advice and real-life example, with practical checklists of what to do to avoid or minimise trouble.

Lastly, Ray Cecil provides a vigorous discussion of the injustices of the present system and describes the changes the future should bring.

Contents
An outline of the law
The main areas of risk
Minimising the impact
Something has to change

'What the practitioner has been waiting for: a book written by an experienced practising architect and one who, by his own account, has been through the fire. It is well researched, and written in a highly readable style . . . I have no hesitation in saying that every practising architect should have a copy of this book.'

The Architects' Journal

234 × 148 mm   *172 pp*   *ISBN 0–85139–956–8*   *cloth*

Contractor's Claims

David Chappell

No two contractor's claims ever seem to be quite the same; they are a potential source of embarrassment to the architect and need to be understood if they are to be dealt with speedily, accurately and fairly.
This book gives practical guidance on ways to assess and determine a claim, and on what action to take once the decision is reached. Simple flow charts guide the reader through all the principal procedures. Model letters are provided, supporting chapters discuss related issues.
Here is a desk-top companion for working architects; and indeed for contractors too, since it indicates how claims may be most effectively presented. It also points up areas of risk, and outlines the good management measures necessary to minimise the need for claims to arise at all.

Contents
What is a claim?
Roles
Contractor's duties
Evidence
Techniques for dealing with extensions of time
Techniques for dealing with loss and/or expense
Claims from sub-contractors
Liquidated damages, penalties and bonus clauses
Architect's certificates
Employer's decisions

'In a claims-conscious age this is an invaluable book for both the inexperienced and the experienced reader. It is a guide . . . which deals with the subject matter in clear and concise terms.'

The Architects' Journal

210 × 148 mm   136 pp   ISBN 0–85139–778–6   cloth

Legal and Contractual Procedures for Architects

Bob Greenstreet

This is a lucid route-map through the legal and contractual maze of everyday architectural practice. Clear flowcharts, checklists, guides to action, and sample documents enable the reader to find essential information at a glance, without having to study lengthy screeds of text. Where more detailed study might be desired, highly selective bibliographies list the precise references to be consulted on each individual aspect of law.

There has long been a need for a desk-top (or briefcase) manual of this kind, to complement the lengthier and more academic textbooks already in existence. This guide maps out clearly all the tricky paths of architectural practice for both the novice and the experienced traveller.

Contents

The architect and the law	Contract formation
The building industry	The construction phase
The architect in practice	Completion
The design phase	Arbitration

This second edition has been revised to take account of changes in case law and rules affecting professional practice.

'An invaluable book for students and young architects embarking on practice.'

RIBA Journal

210 × 297 mm   *110 pp*   *ISBN 0–85139–369–1*   *paper*

JCT Intermediate Form of Contract: An Architect's Guide

David Chappell and Vincent Powell-Smith

The IFC was welcomed by those who found the longer JCT80 unwieldy for use on contracts larger than those covered by the Minor Works form. Certainly, every architect who has not already done so will need to become familiar with it. Clearly written by two experienced authors, this guide is primarily aimed at the architect: it follows the contract through every stage, using a wealth of explanatory material such as sample letters, action flow charts and comparative tables.

Contents

The purpose and use of IFC84
Contracts compared
Contract documents and insurance
The architect's authority and duties
The contractor's obligations
The employer's powers, duties and rights
The clerk of works
Subcontractors and suppliers
Possession, practical completion, and defects liability
Claims
Payment
Determination
Arbitration
Appendix A: Form of tender and agreement NAM/T
Appendix B: NAM/SC subcontract conditions

234 × 148 mm   *227 pp*   *ISBN 0–85139–885–5*   *cloth*

Professional Indemnity Claims

N. P. G. Thomas

More and more claims are being made against architects. This book is written for the architect who is concerned both to understand the ramifications of these claims and how best to avoid their arising in the first place.

The steps in resolving a claim, either by litigation or by arbitration, are described by following a hypothetical case, and simple language is employed to explain the terms used. The author goes on to point out how professional liabilities may arise; he discusses whether they can be avoided, and explains the working of the professional indemnity insurance industry.

He also draws on his experience of claims and provides a checklist of what to avoid and where to take special precautions. This book offers valuable reading for any architect, whether student or long qualified.

Contents

Litigation in the high court
The alternatives to litigation in the high court
The architect as plaintiff
Professional indemnity insurance
The concept of liability
Common causes of liability and their avoidance

'This is a book to be read by all architects. It avoids legal jargon and tedious description . . . Architects, having read this book, should then keep it as quick reference whenever storm clouds appear on the horizon. It might just help avoid getting very wet.'

Building Design

210 × 148 mm   *99 pp*   *ISBN 0–85139–748–4*   *cloth*

Report Writing for Architects

David Chappell

A large part of an architect's working time is spent in preparing reports. They represent a point of contact between architect and client, and a basis for decision-making, They must ask for a sufficiently active response. They can influence the client's opinion of the architect and the chance of further commissions; and if they confuse fact with opinion, they risk dire legal consequences.

Dr Chappell has experience as an architect in private and public practice, as contracts administrator for a building firm, and as an adviser on conservation.

He discusses when reports are needed, their aims, who is going to read them, and the use of consultants. He lists various types of report, gives advice on their presentation, and lists necessary survey equipment in an appendix.

Contents

'A forceful reminder that clarity and discipline in presentation are as important as the contents of your report . . . will prove extremely useful . . . especially now that, because of the question of liability, it is so important to ensure that you have covered your project to a reasonable depth.'

The Architects' Journal

210 × 148 mm   *126 pp*   *ISBN 0–85139–966–5*   *cloth*

Contractual Correspondence for Architects

David Chappell

This is a book for architects about what to do when things go wrong, and how to avoid common problems in following through a job. By means of a brief commentary and 130 sample letters, the author takes the reader through what sometimes seems the minefield that has to be negotiated from the time of appointment to completion of the project and beyond. A copy of this book to hand in the office will provide a ready solution when unforeseen problems arise.

Following the RIBA Plan of Work, the author provides a route-map which will help architects to avoid many of these problems altogether, and, using the sample letters provided, to deal with the rest simply and straightforwardly.

The book assumes that the JCT Standard Form of Agreement has been used, but alternative recommendations are given for the Agreement for Minor Building Works.

Contents

'Problems can and often do arise on even the most well run contracts . . . every architect knows they do but is rarely given any guidance as to how he should act . . . Essential boardside reading for every architect involved in building contracts, however small or large.'

The Architects' Journal

210 × 148 mm   *218 pp*   *ISBN 0–85139–775–1*   *cloth*